Julian Joseph Overbeck

Catholic orthodoxy and Anglo-Catholicism

A word about intercommunion between the English and the Orthodox Churches

Julian Joseph Overbeck

Catholic orthodoxy and Anglo-Catholicism
A word about intercommunion between the English and the Orthodox Churches

ISBN/EAN: 9783337259549

Printed in Europe, USA, Canada, Australia, Japan

Cover: Foto ©Lupo / pixelio.de

More available books at **www.hansebooks.com**

CATHOLIC ORTHODOXY

AND

ANGLO-CATHOLICISM,

A WORD ABOUT INTERCOMMUNION BETWEEN THE ENGLISH
AND THE ORTHODOX CHURCHES.

BY

J. J. OVERBECK, D.D.

"And he said unto me, Son of man, can these bones live? And I answered, O Lord God, thou knowest."—Ezek. xxxvii. 3.

LONDON:
N. TRÜBNER & CO., 60, PATERNOSTER ROW.
1866.

[*The right of Translation is reserved.*]

JOHN CHILDS AND SON, PRINTERS.

PREFACE.

THERE is a kind of constraining power and agency inherent in Truth; "for we cannot but speak the things which we have seen and heard" (Acts iv. 20). Some may deem it wise not to startle the minds of settled persons by what they term a revolution in Religion. Some may deem it preposterous to oppose the rocky wall of the Church to the wild waves of a certain school of human science and researches. Some may deem it harsh and cruel to hurt the feelings of friends, whose most sacred convictions we attack unreservedly. Oh! it is painful, I know, to disagree with those who are dear to our heart. But Truth is uppermost, and permits no bartering, no deference to circumstances whatever.

I found the Orthodox Church to be the only true Catholic Church, and, consequently, try to bring about a Reunion of the other Christian Churches (chiefly of the English Church) with the Orthodox. About a year ago I wrote a German book ("Die orthodoxe katholische Anschauung, &c.," Halle, 1865) on this subject, and had the satisfaction to hear that it was directly circulated in two Russian translations. A Russian gentleman of high standing and profound theological learning wrote me a letter in which he states: "Mon cœur a été touché par cette franche et loyale confession de vos sentiments *vraiment orthodoxes*..... Vous avez su parfaitement bien deviner *les seuls moyens possibles* pour l'union tant désirée entre l'Orient et l'Occident, et ON PEUT ACCEPTER DE FACTO TOUTES LES CONDITIONS QUE VOUS

AVEZ PROPOSÉES." And another Orthodox, who is at the same time a well known theological author of great merit, wrote: "Ihre Ideen sind *praktisch ausführbar,* und desto kräftiger können sie auf die Gemüther der Freunde der Wahrheit wirken. Ihr Buch hat besonders in Petersburg und Moskau eine warme Aufnahme im Publikum gefunden."

Critical reviews came in, pleasant and unpleasant, as it usually happens in such cases. I only pick out two, one of the Protestant "Theologisches Literaturblatt von Dr. K. Zimmermann" [Darmstadt], which is a pattern of benevolent and gentlemanly dealing; and one of the Roman-Catholic "Chilianeum," whose anonymous author hides himself, as it were, "under the water," reminding me of the Ovidian frogs;

Quanquam sint sub aqua, sub aqua maledicere tentant.

The present book was, while I was writing it, simultaneously translated into Russ by kind and actively sympathizing hands.

I trust the English public will be indulgent to my feeble attempt to express myself in their language, and excuse a foreigner to meddle in their affairs. However, Religion is, I think, a common property of mankind, and nationalities may not form a bar in heavenly things, but are connected by a *bond of solidarity* comprising the whole Catholic world. To re-introduce the English Church into this Catholic Commonwealth was my aim in writing this book, and I hope God will bless my endeavours.

Reading, July 7th, 1866.

CONTENTS.

	PAGE
No Popery! No Protestantism!	1
The Church has its branches	1
Catholicity requires, 1. the full truth, 2. an undoubted Apostolical Succession	2
— and, 3. a formal Intercommunion between the several branches of the Church. Insulation is Death	3
The Anglican Church: 1. the Evangelical party	3
2. The Broad Church	4
The Broad-Churchmen more consistent than the Evangelicals	6
Hopes and expectations from the Broad-Churchmen, and the Evangelicals	9
The High Church	12
Her Catholic claims but Protestant associations	13
Providential mission of the Dissenters	15
Church authority	17
New life in the High Church	17
Anglo-Catholics. Ritualists	18
Attitudinarians, Latitudinarians, Platitudinarians	19
Archdeacon Denison and the Ritualists	20
Dr. Pusey. Tractarian movement	20
Dr. Neale	21
I. Do the Anglo-Catholics possess the full Catholic belief?	22
1. What is the relation between the Bible and the Church?	22

CONTENTS.

	PAGE
2. The Anglican notion of the Church is not Catholic	27
3. The Invocation of Saints a binding Catholic doctrine	30
The Church is *triune*, and is inseparably linked by a *Solidarity* of interests (Communion of Saints)	33
Objections : Mr. Archer Gurney	37
St. Epiphanius on the Collyridians	38
The Anglo-Catholics have *no Unity of belief*	40
Mr. S. C. Malan and Dr. Fraser	41
The *Confessio Orthodoxa* on the Invocation of Saints	44
Strong language of the Orthodox formularies	46
On Superstition	50
Papism has apostatized from Catholic Orthodoxy	53
The Russian Church	54
The Raskol. The Stoglaff	55
Mr. Allies	56
The Western Orthodox Catholic Church	59
II. The pretended Apostolical Succession in the English Church	60
Anglican presbyters not ordained by a bishop	61
St. Athanasius and Ischyras	65
Deficient Form in M. Parker's consecration	67
The Roman doctrine on the sacrament of Order is Orthodox	70
The Catholic Bishop contrasted to the Anglican	71
Intercommunion	72
No doctrinal Unity in the English Church	74
Macaulay	75
The Archbishop of Canterbury	77
Dr. Pusey's Organic Church-life	78
Dissection of a passage of Dr. Pusey's Eirenicon	81
Dr. Pusey withdraws into the dark recess of Mysticism	87
" Presbyterians *have* what *they* believe " ?	88
If all the Anglican Bishops proved to be Intercommunionists, what then ?	89
May the Orthodox Church enter into transactions with the English Church at large ?	89
The English Church tolerates heresy	90
Heresy of the Broad Church	90
Heresy of Evangelicalism. Canon Stowell	91
Ill-assorted elements in the English Church	93

CONTENTS. vii

	PAGE
The chief care of the Orthodox Church is to watch the pure Catholic faith	95
She stood firm in affliction and temptation	95
Efforts to bring about an Intercommunion	99
" Deferring all dogmatical debates "	100
The American Episcopal Church and Orthodoxy	101
Awkward dilemma of the Intercommunionists	103
The Russian Church not a State engine	104
"The Churchman's " Jesuitism in the Orthodox Church	106
" Why this move in the direction of the Russian Church ? "	107
Naïveté of the Anglicans, trying to unite Papists, Anglicans, and Orthodox	108
The future Orthodox Anglican Church	108
The Anglo-Catholics cannot represent the English Church	109
Dr. Pusey represents *only a school of opinion*	110
Union between Dr. Pusey and the Evangelicals	111
No Intercommunion but Reunion !	112
The innate Traditional disposition of the English mind	113
Luther	113
The English people did not introduce Reformation	114
The Anglo-Catholics' propensity to Rome	115
ROMANISM. The schism dividing the East and the West contrasted to the Protestant schism	116
The fatal wound of Roman-Catholicism is Papacy	117
The doctrine of St. Peter being the Rock on which the Church is built, was *imported and not developed*	118
Dr. Newman's "faint outlines," and Mr. Allies' "Guardianship of the Vine"	121
This " Guardianship " to be interpreted by Canon XXVIII. of the Council of Chalcedon	122
COMMENTARY on Dr. Newman's "faint outlines"	123
St. Clement bishop of Rome	123
St. Ignatius of Antioch	127
St. Polycarp. Marcion	129
Pope Soter	130
The Montanists. Praxeas	133
Pope Victor and the Asian Churches	135
St. Irenæus. Tertullian	137

	PAGE
St. Dionysius of Alexandria. The Emperor Aurelian	147
St. Cyprian, Pope Stephen	154
On the interpolation and corruption of the Fathers	154
Krabinger's critically revised text	160
The Orthodox notion of the lawful Primacy in the Catholic Church	162
Doom of Papacy from the mouth of St. Cyprian	172
Scrutiny of the Fathers interpreting St. Matthew xvi. 18	172
Dr. Newman's "cumulative argument" collapses	176
Papal Supremacy took its rise from Ambition	177
Tactics of the Jesuits in bringing out the last dogma of the Immaculate Conception of the B. V.	179
The practical working of the Roman system	187
Alfonso de Liguori	188
Dr. Newman's reserve, and Archbishop Manning's explicit teaching	190
Inscription in the Church of S.S. Pudente e Pudenziana	191
Pope Benedict XIV. on Indulgences	192
Spiritual tyranny of Rome	194
Corporeal tyranny of Rome. Pius' Encyclical and Syllabus	194
Cyriaque Zampryllos	195
Mystery of Rome's attractiveness	196
The next step	197
Outlines of the Constitution of the Orthodox Catholic Church of the West	198
Conclusion	200

CATHOLIC ORTHODOXY.

The Catholic truth has been preserved by the Orthodox Catholic Church, whilst Roman Catholicism introduced innovations both in doctrine and discipline into the old common deposit of truth. "*No Popery*" was a cry raised in the East five centuries before the Reformation propagated it to the West. "*No Popery! No Protestantism!*" is *our* cry, and we hope to awake all who seek after truth based on a solid foundation, based on *the Church* which Christ founded and not man.

The Church has *many branches*. There is an Eastern Orthodox Catholic Church, and there is a Western Orthodox Catholic Church (although now disfigured by Romish errors, but to be purified and restored by God's help). Within the Eastern Church there is a Greek, a Russian Church. Within the restored Orthodox Catholic Church of the West there will be an Italian, a Gallican, a Germanic, an Anglican Church. Every nationality will have its Catholic Orthodox Church according to its national usages, but based on the common Catholic doctrine and holy canons.

Without the *full truth* there can be no claim to Catholicity. He who accepts one truth and denies the other, or sticks to one truth as being fundamental, and dispenses with others as being accessory, or unimportant, or doubtful, or even injurious to sound belief—such a one is no Catholic.

Without undoubted *Apostolical Succession* and lawful priesthood there can be no claim to Catholicity. Christ charged his Apostles to teach and to administer the Sacraments. The Apostles consecrated Bishops to do the same. The Bishops ordained Priests and Deacons to assist them in this their work. No others were ever considered by the Church as competent to fulfil this task. Sacerdotal power is from God, not from man. If any one holds all the doctrines of the Church, but depends on an unlawful and invalid Episcopate, his belief cannot supply nor make good the invalidity of Ordination. There will be no Consecration of the Eucharist, no Absolution, &c., since the pretended priest is nothing but a layman.

These general principles will be found correct by every so called Anglo-Catholic. Let us now go a step farther and examine, whether *Catholic Unity can subsist without* FORMAL *Intercommunion between the branches of the Church.*

An *invisible* Intercommunion amounts, in its significance, exactly to an *invisible* Church. But inasmuch as a visible Church has been founded by Christ, a visible Intercommunion is so materially necessary to the Catholic Commonwealth, that an attempt to deny or destroy it would be tantamount to apostasy from Catholicity. Even the wish to have Intercommunion established, but refusing to adopt the proper means, would be an imperfect velleity and sinful indifference.

Let us impress this truth as deeply as possible on our minds, that *Insulation* is Death, that a limb not connected with the body, not taking part in its functions, not co-operating with the whole, is lifeless. You do not delay with gangrene—a moment lost, perhaps all is lost. With the immortal soul on the brink of eternity there is a *periculum in mora*. If the bulk of the Catholic Church denies you admittance, there must be some strong reason not to be slighted.

Let us now view the *Anglican Church*, and examine whether an Intercommunion between the same and the Orthodox Catholic Church is possible and practicable.

First of all, what is the Anglican Church ? The definition is more than difficult. For if I say, it is that Christian Denomination, the basis of which is the Bible, the Prayer-book, and the Thirty-nine Articles, at once the *Evangelical* party will rise and cry: "The Bible, and the Bible only is our foundation. We disapprove a great deal of what the Prayer-book retained from Popery. No Ritualism, no

Sacerdotalism! No sham of Apostolical Succession! We all are priests. There is no Hierarchy *divino jure*, clergymen and laymen are not essentially different, there is only a distinction for order's sake. *Our* Intercommunion extends to Christendom at large, and needs no formal verdict." Now the Evangelicals form the majority of the English Church ; and they neither miss nor want a formal Intercommunion with the Orthodox Catholic Church.

Another party in the English Church, almost as strong as the Evangelicals, and daily gaining a greater ascendency, are the *Broad-Churchmen*. Their belief is like the rainbow, many-coloured, hazy, shaded, clouded, changing according to the temporary taste and fashion. While the Evangelicals are trampling on the Mitre and Crosier, attacking Baptismal Regeneration; Confession, and Real Presence, but fighting for the Bible and its Plenary Inspiration, the Broad-Churchmen pitifully smile at the Evangelical war against Popish trifles, concentrate their force against the Bible, and do not accept but a few "truths sifted from amongst a heap of rubbish hitherto considered as sacred relics." But, in the end, Broad-Churchism evaporates in Pilate's saying : " What is truth ? ! " Well, what is truth ? I ask you. They shrug their shoulders and point to the light of Scientific Researches, shining forth from Preadamite human skeletons, from the vertebral knot of an ape's skull, from the extent of physical and ethnographical studies. Well then let us live to see Christianity crumbling down under the hammer of such powerful miners! They have already, by their watery arguments, quenched "the fire that never shall be quenched," changing eternal punishment into temporal correction. Judas Iscariot, nay, Satan (provided they admit his real existence), will be saved one day. They will be able, I expect, to wield the Cyclopean hammer, forging thunders more effectual than those of the Vatican, in order to smash the Church to pieces. They will be able, I expect, to climb and force, with Titanic bravery, the pinnacles of heaven in order to dethrone the good old Christian God, and to replace him by their weak sentimental phantom of a Deity moulded out of goodness without holiness and justice, a Deity encompassed by a *Magna Charta* of human rights, versus divine usurpations, a Deity of "limited liability." Broad-Churchism strikes at the very root of Christianity. And do you think, after this, that Broad-Churchmen really care a bit for Intercommunion between the Orthodox and English Churches? They like to be left alone; they have no wish to be bothered in their state of perfect ease and comfort; and if they do wish for any Intercommunion at all, it is not with Christians only, not with Jews and Mahommedans only, but with Parsees, Hindoos, and Zulu-Kaffers (as soon as properly educated). Why should we intrude upon Churchmen who consider it the greatest glory of the English Church, that she is so spacious as to accommodate all shades of religious opinions; that she is not so narrow-minded as to exclude any newcomer, or to ask him after his Christian credentials. This forcibly reminds me of the large barrack-like Parisian "Cités" which accommodate hundreds of families without any other mutual bond but the bare walls of the building.

There is, however, a grand and prominent feature in Broad-Churchism, the undoubted merits of which claim our just appreciation. *The Broad-Churchmen are the only consistent Protestants* as opposed to the Evangelicals. They alone can boast of standing on the genuine ground of the Reformation, sticking fearlessly to the right of Private Judgment, which Luther so emphatically claimed for himself, but denied to others.

Si fractus illabatur orbis,
Impavidum ferient ruinæ.

Never mind the ruins they make; the ruins are but the necessary process of dissolution. Bishop Colenso speaks out what he thinks, and he may do so, for Protestantism has no lawful authority to restrain Private Judgment. The Evangelicals lament the awful mischief which this modern school of unbelief produces. And so do we. They invite us to combat our common enemy. And so do we. They call their opponents traitors to the Protestant cause. And we do not, for Broad-Churchmen are the only true Protestants. They bewail the decline of belief, but glory in Protestantism. We bewail the decline of belief, but still more bewail Protestantism as being the real parent of this unbelief. They pray God to protect and uphold Protestantism. We consider such prayer a blasphemy, and pray for the destruction of Protestantism. We hail Broad-Churchmen as the destroying angels of Protestantism. We congratulate them on every breach they make in the Protestant stronghold, not for their sapping the Christian belief, but for bringing the malady of Protestantism to a wholesome crisis. Dr. Strauss and Dr. Schenkel fling contemptuous inconsistency into the face of their Evangelical opponents. The Evangelicals produce the Bible, but their adversaries challenge them to demonstrate its genuineness, authenticity, and inspiration, but they cannot, on Protestant ground, stand the force of their opponents' arguments, they resort to the Church and its Traditions, call History to their assistance, viz. Church-witnesses. The Broad-Churchmen reply: "That is foul play! Don't apply to the Church, the pillars of which the Samsons of the Reformation have effectually shaken and upset!" Thus the Evangelicals dwindle away into nothingness, execrate the enemy with unctuous animosity and stubborn fanaticism. Voilà tout! Arguments they have not on Protestant ground, but holy indignation, prophetic thunders, and cheap sneers.

Difficile est, satiram non scribere.

The Evangelicals float in the air without any solid ground to rest upon. The Bible they have purloined from the Church. Therefore it is a lifeless and deadly letter in their hands, a letter which they twist according to their moderate measure of understanding or misunderstanding. Not two Evangelicals together understand the most important passages of the Bible in the same way. They slide over precipices, unwilling to expose themselves in sounding the depths. And then they swear the clearness and sufficiency of the book, which they have overclouded by a mist of human effusions. The mist they like, it is true, because they cannot reach the ground under their feet. Visionary prophecies and sublime hallucinations about them fill their souls, but the true ground they lose sight of.

This *true ground* is the Church, the one Catholic and Apostolic Church which historically continued since Pentecost. From this Church Protestantism snatched the Bible, but lost (together with the Church) its legitimation and the key to its understanding.

Our sympathy is with neither of the parties, but if Consistency is a plea for preference, we decide in favour of the Broad-Churchmen. Although the Evangelicals are believers and hold a great many more truths in common with the Catholic Church (chiefly the truth of Christ the God-Man and his Atonement), than the Broad-Churchmen, those truths are either enveloped in a cloud of incorrect notions, or partly altered and falsified, and, in the end, the whole structure rests upon as wrong a basis as the Broad Church; with the exception, that a sect of fanatic believers is much less accessible to truth and resipiscence than a sect of scanty belief and broad rationalism. The Broad Church is a blank, a *tabula rasa ;* the Evangelical Low Church is a prolific, luxurious field covered with lianas and weeds, stifling the few flowers and fruits which occasionally may be produced.

And now, *what are our hopes and expectations from these two parties of the English Church?*

The Evangelicals scarcely will yield by themselves to any plan of Orthodox Intercommunion. Their inveterate self-conceit can only be broken, as it were, by a wonder. They display great activity, have a fervent love for the Bible, and a fervent hatred of all that contradicts their opinions. They do not love *the* Bible, but *their* Bible. After having infused into the Bible their misconceptions, they like this *their subjective* Bible, cherishing in the Bible nothing but their own conceited *self*, fondling their biblicized Calvin. They read the Bible, are fond of the Bible, as being *their home-made book*, not as the God-sent Church-book. I call this an egotistical worship; I call this—*Bibliolatria*. They love Christ, and Dr. Pusey forgives them a great many errors on account of their love of Christ. But "if any man shall say unto you, Lo, here is Christ, or there; believe it not; for there shall arise false Christs." I openly confess that I dislike a Calvinistic Christ, and that I do not "go forth into the desert to see him." I only like *the true, historical Christ of the Church*, not the heretical phantom of Christ, preaching Calvin's doctrines—and awful doctrines they are—subverting the very foundation of all Catholic truth, haunting poor mankind and hunting them into despair for three centuries past. Such a Christ was not crucified for us; he cannot atone us, because he sprang from the brains of Calvin, but did not descend from heaven. "But they intend at least to love the real Christ, and their good intention will save them." I hope so myself, however the idolater also intends to worship the real God, not the brass or ivory idol, but the hidden God, represented by those images, and still nobody doubts his idolatry. I will not carry this momentous question any farther, but content myself with hinting how deeply Protestantism has uprooted the Christian truth.

The Broad-Churchmen are quite bewildered, frightened out of their wits, haunted by our "portentous" notion of an "*infallible Church.*" And how could they catch the idea, after having lost the *Personality of the Holy Ghost?* Church-infallibility is, therefore, in their eyes associated with priestcraft on the one hand, and with outright folly on the other hand. They write on the Church doors:

> Per me si va nella città dolente:
> Per me si va nell' eterno dolore:
> Lasciate ogni speranza voi, che 'ntrate.

Still they cannot refrain from staring at this imposing fabric of astounding consistency. "*Consistency*" is the spell which charms these men and introduces them into the study of the Catholic Church. They study, grow more and more interested in the matter, and finish by finding the commensurability of our notions, their rationality, their cogency. How many earnest Rationalists have joined the Church, even some of their most desperate leaders, e. g. Daumer! Others are paving the way to the Church, e. g. Bruno Bauer. In this question experience can only show on which side there is a greater hope for the Church; and I think, experience points to those wanderers, poor in belief, whose lives are spent in seeking the truth, not in enjoying the riches of self-made truths. The honest Rationalists are nearer the truth than the boastful Evangelicals, who do not search the Scriptures but for finding supports of their own tenets; and when Scripture clashes with their preconceived notions, Scripture must yield to the most painful contortions. The Evangelical is the rich and pious Pharisee, the Broad-Churchman is the poor, needful, doomed Publican in our Saviour's parable. Hence you will scarcely see a determined Evangelical join the Catholic Church, but he rather associates with the Irvingites or the Plymouth Brethren or any other mystical sect, tired even of the easy shackles of the English Church.

One finds, however, among Evangelicals a band of truly humble souls, poor in spirit, without bitterness and animosity, not spasmodically clinging to a sectarian creed, but open to the light from above. These are dear to our heart, and we pray that, as they already *implicitè* belong to the Catholic fold, God in his mercy may soon lead them to the visible communion with our Church.

On the contrary, there is a large class of Broad-Churchmen, chiefly consisting of young worldly people of loose morals or superficial scientific pursuits, who use or rather abuse religion as a cloak which one needs in good society; or who use Religion as a butt for their abortive wits and loathsome sneers. There is no human hope for these, but the heavy hand of God's merciful providence may, in due season, find its way to the heart of those whom we consider now to be castaways.

Summing up the result of the preceding pages we find:

1. That neither the Evangelicals nor the Broad-Churchmen have a proper notion of "*the Church*" in the Catholic meaning of the word;

2. That both parties do not recognize an *obligatory Church-authority*;

3. That they do neither wish nor want an Intercommunion of the English and Orthodox Churches;

4. That the Orthodox Church must declare them to be heretics, with whom an Intercommunion would not only be impossible, but positively sinful, since by such Intercommunion heresy and schism would creep into the Orthodox Church, and would make her Heterodox, depriving her of all farther claim to Catholicity.

The third party of the English Church is called *High-Church*. They form, so to say, the *Conservative body* of the Church, whereas the Evangelicals may be termed to a certain extent the *Liberals*, and the Broad-Churchmen the *Radicals*. These High-Churchmen lay a stress upon *the Church*, connect the Bible with the Church, respect the old Church-observances, e. g. the vigils, the feast and fast days, which have fallen into utter desuetude with the other parties of the Church. They like to style their clergymen "Priests," and themselves to be considered a branch of the Catholic Church. The Church is their aristocratic pride, and they contribute large sums for building, beautifying, restoring, endowing churches. Hooker's Church Polity is their standard work. You will find on the shelves of those among them who profess theological learning, the works of their Bishops Andrewes, Laud, Beveridge, Bramhall, Overall, Nicholson, Wilson, Cosin, Bull, &c. The Dissenters and their Chapels they disdain, and feel sorely grieved at the Evangelical dissent creeping into the Church. Of the Broad Church they are ashamed, and feel deeply the defect of the English Church in not being able to excommunicate them. They love both the Prayer Book and the Thirty-nine Articles, either not perceiving the deep gulf between both, or bridging it by interpreting the Articles by the Prayer Book, as the Evangelicals interpret the Prayer Book by the Articles. No wonder that both parties, although building on the same substruction, come to a very different result. The chief glory of the High-Churchmen is the boasted Apostolical Succession of their Bishops. They profess not to entertain the least doubt about the same. Still neither the Romish nor the Orthodox Church recognize it, and the Protestants do not care for it. Thus the English Church remains *insulated*. Again, *Insulation* naturally creates uneasiness, doubt, peevishness. How is it that such an immense number of books are written about the Validity of English Ordinations? If the matter is so evident, as you say, it is but time and labour lost to write ever and anon on the same subject. And dangerous it is too to speak so much about a matter till one begins to doubt, who never thought before of doubting. Is it not the same with a defendant who asserts his innocence but cannot come to an end in asserting it? At last people begin to think there must be a hitch in the business, he cannot feel re-assured himself, else he would not continue re-assuring others. It is a sad thing to be insulated, without relations, friends, or acquaintances. In fact, it is so uncommon that one feels obliged to ask, why is it so? The Protestants alone are the only persons who offer their friendship and intercommunion, but you refuse for fear of embarking in an affair by which you might lose your Catholic claims. Thus all the Catholic world refuse Intercommunion with you, re-ordain your priests who join their Church, and have continued doing so for the last three centuries? A long time indeed! Is it not hoping against hope to flatter oneself with finally obtaining a favourable decision in a controversy pending so long, a controversy which *in its practical bearing* has been decided in the negative? For how could the Catholics re-ordain your priests *unconditionally*, if they entertained even the remotest doubts about the Invalidity of your Ordinations, or if they did not consider the question as finally and peremptorily settled ? However, you have one small friend, *the Moravian Episcopal Church.* You recognize each other, *consequently you adopt the full Protestant creed of the Augsburg Confession,* on which the Moravians rest. Now we want another Newman to show the harmony of the Thirty-nine Articles and the Augsburg Confession. It would not be difficult, I am sure; at least not so difficult as that clever feat to harmonize the Thirty-nine Articles and the Tridentine Confession. At all events it would be worth while trying to reconcile the Augsburg with the Tridentine Confession by the instrumentality and mediation of the Thirty-nine Articles. Romanism and Protestantism, fire and water reconciled !

There exists a Caricature representing an elderly, sleepy bishop on the box of an omnibus, driving on slowly, very slowly. On the opposite side you see the Baptist Spurgeon, riding on the steam-engine of an express-train, with flying hair, riding and preaching all along. It is not very pleasant, indeed, to be joked at, but as long as the joke is not a mere calumny, there is some truth at the bottom which one ought to mind.

Ridendo dicere verum.

Lord Palmerston had a very fine collection of his caricatures, and, no doubt, he had improved by them, the legitimate legatees of the prince's jesters. Let us now inquire into the truth of the picture. The Baptists, the most active, restless, turbulent

Dissenters, essentially akin to the Evangelicals within the pale of the English Church, represent the stirring element in the religious world, stirring, ever stirring, without settling. It is interesting to see a high-spirited youth rushing out to conquer the world. By his noise he arouses people from sleep; by his endless talk he molests quiet men and compels them to lift their voices; by his importune questioning he drives one mad, but in the end you answer his questions, in order to be relieved from the inquisitive young man. His voluble tongue utters a great deal of trash, of florid nonsense, it is true, but among the rubbish you will find sometimes a hidden pearl, a word which strikes home, arousing the heedless sleeper from a dangerous security. The young man rides off on the steam-engine, but your sleep is gone, you feel uneasy, unsettled, doubts have entered your mind. .... That is the *Providential Mission* of the Dissenters and their Evangelical friends in the English Church, to awaken their brethren from a sound, but dangerous sleep. They rested on the downy pillow of an unattackable, unconquerable Church, providing for them plenty of food, both spiritual and corporeal, plenty of truth, plenty of salvation —and all this at the cheapest prices, i. e. with the least trouble and exertion.—Once the English Church was a spell—now this spell is broken—it is like a rich man who in the midst of his riches feels poor and troubled in the very hall of his mediæval palace, surrounded by his glorious ancestors gazing from the gilt-framed pictures!

The watchword of the Conservative High-Churchman is: "*Rest and be thankful!*" An infallible Church and strong Church-authority would be just the thing for them. Unfortunately this authority is invested in a king or queen who may possibly follow Broad-Church advice or listen to Evangelical schemes. This authority is limited or rather exercised by the Parliament, full of hostile elements, eager to weaken or destroy the Church. The soul of the Parliament is the weather-cock called "*Public Opinion*," a rather inconstant regulator of divine things. But is there not the National Church Council "Convocation" discussing Church affairs? Yes, it is discussing—that is all. Binding resolutions it cannot issue, save by act of Parliament. And in this Convocation Low, Broad, and High-Churchmen are sitting and debating, truly a most unpromising *mixtum compositum* of heterogeneous principles. — Let us pass by this ominous flaw in the Church-fabric!

There was a time when the English Church possessed a strange, unenvied power, viz. the "*Vis inertiæ*," slumbering on into broad daylight. The Dissenters were moving and stirring—infidelity, indifference, immorality revelling—Wesley crying and pulling his mother-church, till she awoke; but more than one third of the Church was gone. She awoke imbued with new life, ever since keeping up with the times—but this life was, like sectarian life, merely individual. However, this High Church displays a show of Church-life, which points at least to a want of *real* Church-life. The High Church combats manlily heretical teaching in the teeth of Low Church (Gorham case), Broad Church (Essays and Reviews, Bishop Colenso), and Parliament; and although defeated, repeatedly defeated, legally defeated, she glories in her defeat for Christ's sake. Alas, it is the Constitution of their Church which allowed them to be defeated by heresy. Do you not see that you are fighting against your own Church, which has become a refuge of heresy? Or is there any safeguard of sound belief within the Church? Can you disown the heretical Churchmen sitting at your side in the Council of the Church, preaching from your pulpits, teaching your children, thus instilling the venom of heresy into the hearts of the rising generation in whose hands lies the destiny of times to come? These heretical Churchmen are protected by the law; they live on your loaves and fishes, and would laugh at your attempt to excommunicate them. Again, let us pass by this ominous flaw in the Church-fabric!

Within the High Church there is a party who see "the abomination of desolation stand in the holy place," who lift up their eyes and look out for comfort and help, for strength and power, for rest and peace. They open the Catholic annals of old, consult the fathers of the Church, meditate in the Lives of the Saints. A new light dawns upon them. Happy hours are spent with S. Basil, Chrysostom, Augustine. "Well, let us again infuse their life into our Church!" A fuller belief is wrought out, scanty articles filled with substantial truth, long-forgotten sacraments re-introduced, ascetic life resuscitated. Excellent men they are these earnest High-Churchmen. Would all the High Church were of the same stamp, but a good number of its members are nothing but mere Conservatives, and do not take the trouble to go beyond their actual church, whilst others, in premature haste, precipitate beyond the mark, delight in trifles, decorations, pompous garments, trimming up of churches, minute observances. They ransack Romsey and Bona, and astonish their people by their abstruse ritualistic learning rather than edify the same. They think to have our sympathy, since their innovations are but old Catholic usages gleaned in the East and chiefly in the West. But *on the Catholic ground* these usages are significant, instructive, wholesome, having historically grown up in their genuine soil. On the contrary, transplanted into a cold, heterogeneous soil, they die away or grow into superstition. These Ritualists play at ceremonies like children, forgetting that the soul is more than the body, and both more than the dress. It is a common mistake to take this class of Churchmen as representatives of the High Church. They are, not inappropriately, termed in a certain paper "*Attitudinarians*," as opposed to the "*Latitudinarians*" (Broad-Churchmen) and "*Platitudinarians*" (Evangelical Low-Churchmen). These ALP are indeed "*der Alp*" (the incubus) of the English Church. Against those Attitudinarians

Archdeacon Denison is the able exponent of High-Church principles. In the Norwich Church Congress ("the Churchman," Oct. 12, 1865, p. 1184) he said: "he did feel that in this country they were in a dangerous position on account of a disposition *to introduce too much of ultra ritualism*—of observances which, after all, were only the exponents of a high state of doctrine *which had been painfully arrived at*, and which could never be put in the place of the teaching of the doctrine. No greater mistake could be made than for a man to say, 'I am going to teach my people doctrine by wearing certain vestments and using certain forms.' It would be a happy thing to go through the land and be able to see no clergyman vested in any way but in that to which all eyes had been accustomed. He had the utmost regard and respect for many of those who differed from him on the subject, because he knew that among them there were many of the most painstaking and hard-working of God's Ministers, and therefore he desired to deal with the subject tenderly. At the same time, he could not doubt *that they were committing a great mistake.*"

The real head of the most respectable High-Churchmen is *Dr. Pusey*, whose profound learning and deep Christian humility, together with his unflinching courage amidst persecutions and sneers, deserve our admiration and sympathy. He has such a truly Catholic turn in his mode of thinking that we wonder how he does not feel uneasy in a

Church beset with so many obstacles, open to heresy, devastated within, broken up from without. It must be, no doubt, on the one hand the force of habit which keeps him in a Church, in which he was born and educated. On the other hand, he must foster an idea of his Church, which idea is far from real, but which the love of his mother-church realizes to his heart. Do we not see thousands of affectionate children who cannot see (and if they could, they may not see) the defects of their mother which everybody else sees? Dr. Pusey is the father of the so-called *Anglo-Catholics*, sometimes styled *Puseyites*, though by this by-name are generally understood those High-Churchmen who revel in decorative tom-fooleries and stylish ceremonies. He was, though not the originator, still a mighty support of the *Tractarian* movement. He quieted the passions of the young hot-brained Tractarians, smoothed down the Romanizing tendencies, and was always an upright friend of the Eastern Church, which he considered to be in unison with his own. Still he remained a Western Churchman, guided by the true idea that both Churches are fully entitled to have their own way and subsistence, only linked by the bond of common Catholic truth and Catholic Constitution. He would be quite right, provided his Church were a true branch of the Western Catholic Church. The same is the case with Dr. Neale's most excellent lecture, "The Bible, and the Bible only, the religion of Protestants," which is quite unexceptionable if you substitute "Catholic Church" for "English Church." Dr.

Neale's *ideal* English Church is equally opposed to Popery and Protestantism. Would it were so in the *real* English Church. Let a Broad-Churchman of very advanced principles approach Dr. Neale's communion-table—will he be able, lawfully, to refuse him the communion? Let the Bishop of London enter his chapel and see his half Eastern, half Western sacerdotal garments—what do you think would be his episcopal verdict?

Now let us inquire into the claim of the Anglo-Catholics to be members of the Catholic Church.

I.

Do the Anglo-Catholics possess the full Catholic belief?

If we must decide in the negative, it will be sufficient to prove that *some* of the fundamental Catholic truths are *not* held by the Anglo-Catholics, without entering into an examination of the other unsound doctrines.

In acceding to Archbishop Manning's charge, that " the Church of England rejects *much* Christian truth," we specify this charge by singling out the most advanced believing party of the English Church, showing that even those cannot claim Catholicity of belief.

1. *What is the relation between the Bible and the Church?*

In order to simplify this question, let me propose the respective Orthodox Catholic view.

Jesus Christ taught his Apostles, during his lifetime *and* from his Resurrection to his Ascension, *all* the Catholic truth, founded *the Church*, to be guided infallibly by the indwelling Holy Ghost, "upon the foundation of the apostles and prophets, Jesus Christ himself being the chief corner-stone." THIS CHURCH IS "THE PILLAR AND GROUND OF THE TRUTH,"—and I add most emphatically—the ONLY pillar and ground of the truth. The Apostles deposited this truth in their several Churches, consecrated bishops to be their successors and preservers of the truth deposited. Of this "*depositum fidei*" part was occasionally written, part orally transmitted (2 Thess. ii. 15), but both the written and unwritten word of God formed but one and the same faith, the faith of the Church. This *One Word of God*, as contained in Bible and Tradition, cannot be torn asunder without making the Bible a storehouse of deadly weapons, a refuge of heresy, a hand-book for the use of Satan (St. Matt. iv. 6). The Bible is *neither the complete nor sufficient source of Christian truth*, but explicitly points to the contrary. To the apostles Jesus Christ " shewed himself alive after his passion by many infallible proofs, being seen of them forty days, and speaking of the things pertaining to the kingdom of God" (Acts i. 3). What did he speak during those *forty days* ? "About the things pertaining to the kingdom of God," i. e. about the *Constitution of the Church* and *Church-doctrine.* And quite natural it was, for the foundation of the Church was close at hand. Of this teaching we find fragments scattered about in the Epistles, as occasion required it, but nowhere is written down the complete account of the preparatory instruction which Christ gave his Apostles in the days between his Resurrection and Ascension. Still the Church rests on this instruction, completing what we do not find in the Bible. For instance, nobody can satisfactorily settle the important question of the Baptism of infants from the Bible. Without the teaching of my Church I certainly should be in this point a Baptist. Again, according to Catholic Church teaching, the *seven* Sacraments are instituted by Christ himself; but, in the Bible, you can only find two sacraments instituted by Christ. Therefore you make the heterodox distinction of two essentially different classes of sacraments, viz. the two *real* sacraments, Baptism and the Lord's Supper, and five sacramental rites of minor importance. Consistently you can attach to the latter class only an "*operatio ex opere operantis,*" and if you still assert an "*operatio ex opere operato,*" it is but one of the many inconsistencies which overcloud Anglo-Catholicism vibrating between Church and Bible. We have the Church *including* the Bible, both forming but one *Unity*. You have the Bible *and* the Church, forming a *Duality* disparaging either of the two. Now as you hold the genuine Protestant belief of the *self-subsistence* of the Bible, not considering the Bible as a fruit of the Church in the full Catholic meaning of the word, *exclusively* belonging to the Church, to be interpreted *only* by the Church —you cannot find the proper position of the Church, but place her under the control of the Bible. I say, you do not fully consider the Bible as a fruit of the Church, which fruit, as soon as ripe, i.e. canonically completed and universally recognized, was detached from the tree, became *self-supporting* and *sovereign*, though not directly hostile to the tree which retains the office of keeping the Bible's Pedigree, after having been superseded by the Bible in all its other primitive functions. Before the Bible was ready, the Church was acknowledged to have been an absolute monarch; since the Bible is ready, the Church became (in the opinion of Protestants) a constitutional prince, lodged in a splendid palace, but bereaved of all rights, even of the right of Veto. The real power lies with the Magna Charta of the Bible, which every one twists as it pleases him. It is true, the Church is a most convenient *armoury* for the Anglo-Catholics to find weapons for defending themselves and combating Protestantism, but they forget that the primitive position of the Church is *materially altered*, since the Bible ceased to be the Church's helpmate, both (Church and Bible) being but one and the same organ of the Holy Ghost. Since the Reformation the Bible has to watch over the Church, and has to dictate the sound belief to the Church. Now I call this *Protestant table-turning.* Such a Church *beside the Bible* (instead of the Bible *within* the Church) may be useful, handy, comfortable, but she is *not necessary*, merely " un article de luxe." Wherefore the greater bulk of consistent Protestants exploded the antiquated idea of the Church as being both cumbrous and injurious to pure Bible-belief.

The English Church teaches on this point in the 6th and 20th of the 39 Articles: "Holy Scripture containeth *all* things necessary to salvation: so that whatsoever is not read therein, nor may be proved thereby, *is not to be required of any man*, that it should be believed as an article of the Faith, or be thought requisite or necessary to salvation." "The Church hath power to decree Rites or Ceremonies, and authority in Controversies of Faith (? !): and yet it is not lawful for the Church *to ordain anything that is contrary to God's Word written, neither may it so expound one place of Scripture, that it be repugnant to another*. Wherefore, although the Church be a witness and a keeper of Holy Writ, yet, *as it ought not to decree anything against the same*, so besides the same ought it not to enforce anything to be believed for necessity of Salvation." Now I think this is *Doctrina Protestantissima*,* and I really pity those Anglo-Catholics who endeavour to interpret into these articles even the smallest amount of Catholic truth. Dr. Pusey candidly owns this Protestant doctrine, defends this *Sufficiency of Holy Scripture* (Eiren. pp. 38, 39), and, therefore, stands on genuine Protestant ground. Newman (Tract xc. 1865, p. 8), although acknowledging the meaning

* *Jeremy' Taylor* inscribes the 2nd Section, Book I. Part II. of his "Dissuasive from Popery" (Oxford, 1836), p. 187: "Of the sufficiency of the Holy Scriptures to Salvation, *which is the great foundation and ground of the Protestant religion.*" The reason why the Scriptures are sufficient to salvation is too *naïve* not to be given in the Bishop's own words (l. c. p. 188) : "That the Scripture is a full and sufficient rule to Christians in faith and manners, a full and perfect declaration of the will of God, *is therefore certain*, BECAUSE WE HAVE NO OTHER."

of the above articles to be "that it (the Church) derives the faith *wholly from Scripture*," does not seem to agree with them, quoting a passage from Field's work on the Church (p. 11): "So then, *we do not make Scripture the Rule of our Faith*, but that other things in their kind are Rules likewise; in such sort that *it is not safe*, without respect had unto them, *to judge things by the Scripture alone.*" And Newman himself sums up the result of his researches by the words (p. 12): "Scripture, it is plain, is *not*, on Anglican principles, the Rule of Faith."

2. *The Anglican notion of the Church is not Catholic.*

Since Protestantism has *nominally* emancipated the Bible from the pretended bondage of the Church, the Church (i. e. their Church) lost the domain of authoritative doctrinal teaching, i. e. *Infallibility.* You may screw up the authority of the Church as high as possible, you never will attain Infallibility, because the *quantitativè* superlative of human authority is *qualitativè* differing from Divine Infallibility. The English Church never aspired to the doctrine of Church-Infallibility, but teaches the contrary, that "it is not lawful for the Church to ordain anything that is contrary to God's Word written, neither may it so expound one place of Scripture that it be repugnant to another." Again, "it ought not to decree anything against the same (i. e. Holy Writ)," and "besides the same ought it not to enforce anything to be believed for necessity of Salvation." Of course any *particular*

Church is liable to error, but the 20th Article speaks of *the Church* in general, designating her as "witness and keeper of Holy Writ," which implies the whole body of the Catholic Church. And still this fallible Church is said to have "authority in Controversies of Faith." Bishop Mant (in his annotated edition of the Prayer-Book, p. 777, *seq.*) gives the following illustration of this Church-authority after the Bishops Burnet and Tomline: "It appears from the preceding Article, that it is not here intended *to ascribe to the Church an infallible authority*. . . . . But this, however, we may observe, that, *without any pretension to infallibility*, and without any infringement of *the right of private judgment*, the Church has power to declare Articles of faith, provided they be authorized by Scripture. . ." Now fancy Articles of faith framed by a fallible Church, introducing heresy and schism. But are not the particular Churches, composing the great One Catholic Church, fallible in their decisions? Yes. Still here see the difference of the Anglican standard. The particular Catholic Churches commune with each other. Their decisions are, by their sister-Churches, tested on the common deposit of Catholic faith. If they stand the test, they are *infallibly* Catholic truths; if not, the respective particular Church must renounce its error, or will be cut off from the body of the Catholic Church. As to the English Church, it stands *insulated*, without any recognized Catholic sister-Church, disowned by the whole Catholic Church, unable to be controlled on the Catholic deposit of faith. Even if all the particular Churches of Catholic Christendom would undertake the difficult task to examine the Anglican belief, their verdict would be invalid, since "things ordained by them (i. e. General Councils representing the whole Catholic Church) as necessary to salvation have *neither strength nor authority*, unless it may be declared that they be taken out of Holy Scripture" (Art. XXI).—It is quite right what Dr. Pusey says (Eiren. p. 40): "The authority of the Church was given to her by her Divine Lord within certain limits. 'Teach them,' He said, 'whatever I command you.' All must admit, then, that she could not command anything which should be really contrary to Holy Scripture. Nor must she contradict herself." But the plain words of the 20th Article imply that the Church (not one or the other of the Churches, but *the Church*) may occasionally "ordain something *that is contrary to God's Word written*," and "*so expound one place of Scripture that it be repugnant to another.*" This being the case, Church-Infallibility is impossible. If the Church *cannot* err in doctrine, consequently *cannot* "ordain anything that is contrary to God's Word written, &c.," no sensible man would frame an article tending to preclude the Church from ill-using the Bible. What would you say, if any Church would make an article: "It is not lawful for *God* to ordain anything that is contrary to God's Word written, &c.?" The negative wording would be true, though unmeaning. Now the Church is the organ of *God* the Holy Ghost. It is, therefore, *not a harmless, but a blasphemous sup-*

position that the Church may teach errors, and contradict or misinterpret the Bible. It is all very well that Dr. Pusey (l. c. p. 37, *seqq.*) pleads the *Divine authority* of the Church, but in doing so he unintentionally censures the 20th Article which " lays down certain limits to it " (p. 39)—*human* limits to *Divine* authority !—*human* safeguards to *Divine* usurpation ! It is awful to think, how many and momentous errors sprang from the vicious notion of the Church which the Reformation introduced, and which the English Church faithfully preserves in her 20th Article. No Anglo-Catholic can honestly elude its meaning, nor deny its bearing on the whole Anglican system of belief.

3. *The Invocation of Saints a binding Catholic doctrine.*

I select this point of difference between the Catholic and English Churches for two reasons: 1st, because it illustrates the Catholic principle that the Bible is *not* sufficient to teach all the Catholic truth ; for from the Bible alone nobody can satisfactorily substantiate that doctrine; although, *in the light of the Church*, there may be easily found a confirmation in Scripture ; 2nd, because it is just now earnestly ventilated in Anglo-Catholic circles. We know there are many Anglo-Catholics who hold this doctrine, treated in an exhaustive manner by Bishop Forbes in his " Considerationes modestæ " as early as the beginning of the 17th century. But some of those who hold this doctrine, do not hold it to its full extent ; some hold it only *theoretically*, but dispense with it *practically;* some deem it true, but a ticklish question too captious for the understanding of the people, and easily leading to superstition; some regard it as private indulgence—but *all* Anglo-Catholics treat the matter as an open question, deny the *vital* importance of this question, and the *necessity* of holding *and practising* it. They refer to the Council of Trent (whose authority the Orthodox Catholic Church does *not* recognize), which only requires to acknowledge that the saints may be invoked profitably, leaving the practical consequences to the discretion of its votaries. But the Orthodox Catholic Church, knowing that no doctrine has been revealed to remain barren, requires with the belief also the practice which only shows that the faith is real and not fictitious. If any one holds the Invocation of saints to be salutary, but does not practise it, unbelief or a want of conviction lurks in the background.

There has been talked a great deal of nonsense upon this subject by persons who did not know the Orthodox Catholic doctrine. They speak of *primary, secondary, oblique Invocation, Comprecation,* &c., barricading themselves against a foe who does not exist within the walls of Catholic Orthodoxy, which always opposed popular superstitions. The whole controversy could have been easily settled, and more deeply understood and valued, if they had only viewed it in the right light, that is to say, if they had seen the connection of this doctrine and that of the *Communion of Saints*, which is almost a dead letter to Protestants, who do not care for the departed, and only stick to the Church Militant.

Let us, therefore, give the outlines of a deeper view of the doctrine.

The Church is the *Body of Christ* (Ephes. i. 23), and "we are members of his body, of his flesh and of his bones" (Ephes. v. 30). Christ is the true Vine, and we are its branches. But this union is not to be understood of a hidden and invisible Church, for "every branch in me that beareth not fruit he taketh away" (St. John xv. 2). Hence the withered branch was also a branch, and consequently the Church, which is spoken of as the body of Christ, is *the visible Church*, whose members are incorporated in Christ by Baptism, and bound to believe his doctrine, and to observe his commandments. This body of Christ is mystically but *really* (not only figuratively) animated by Christ's Spirit (hence the Church's *Infallibility*), pervaded by his own sacramental powers, defended by his Almighty arm. The Church is, as it were, a continued Incarnation of Christ. The Church is " der fortlebende Christus." Christ is her head, her only head (which needs not the paltry representation by a Vicar on earth); she feeds upon Christ; in her veins circulates Christ's blood. Such an aspect of the Church as *Christ's living Organism* must show at once, how the poor, miserable idea of a Zwinglian or Calvinistic Lord's Supper could scarcely find an understanding with the Catholics, who require infinitely more for the support of their life in the Church. Even Luther's Christified Bread, or Impanate Christ, was sure to be exploded by the Church as a kind of Eucharistic Monophysitism.

This Church is *tripartite*, the "Ecclesia Militans" on earth, the "Ecclesia Triumphans" of the departed saints, and the "Ecclesia Laborans" of those who "have departed with faith, but without having had time to bring forth fruits worthy of repentance. St. Basil the Great in his prayers for Pentecost says, that the Lord vouchsafes to receive from us propitiatory prayers and sacrifices *for those that are kept in Hades*, and allows us the hope of obtaining for them peace, relief, and freedom" (The longer Russian Catechism: on the eleventh article of the creed).

This *triune* Church is INSEPARABLY LINKED BY A "SOLIDARITÉ" OF INTERESTS, so that if "one member suffer, all the members suffer with it; or one member be honoured, all the members rejoice with it." "That there should be no schism in the body; but that the members should have the same care one for another" (1 Cor. xii. 26, 25). Such is the wonderful, mysterious vitality of the Church *in* Christ* and *through* Christ, that even the gates of hell cannot prevail against her. Such is her *Penetrancy*, that neither Heaven nor Hades (i. e. Purgatory in the Orthodox meaning of the word) can form a wall of partition. Only between the Church and Hell (where the damned souls, the

---

* Remark the pregnancy of the expression ἐν Χριστῷ (where you would expect εἰς Χριστόν), which superficial commentators interpret as Hellenism instead of εἰς; e. g. 1 Cor. xv. 19 : ἠλπικότες ἐσμὲν ἐν Χριστῷ—the hope arising from the incorporation in Christ.

withered branches, are finally gathered) " there is a great gulf fixed: so that they which would pass from hence to you cannot; neither can they pass to us that would come from thence" (St. Luke xvi. 26).

This is the substance of the doctrine of the "*Communion of Saints,*" a doctrine the bearing of which is boundless, by far exceeding the reach of human thought; a doctrine so comprehensive, so consolatory, so encouraging to Christian energy, and at the same time instilling the deepest humility, that every true Catholic must feel most deeply indebted to the Lord for this his inestimable benefit, so much the more so, as the Protestants have rent the Church which Christ knitted together by an indissoluble bond, have broken the intercourse between the two worlds, and confined themselves to the poor help which the sinful pilgrims here below bring one to another. They say: "God is our only help; Christ is our only mediator; we need nobody else." But who ever doubted the truism you advance? Or do you doubt it yourselves, perhaps, because you ask your brother to pray for you and with you? Or cannot God himself help mankind, since he sends his angels to minister to them? Is it not an unjustifiable mistake of Christ when speaking of the offence of despising the little ones, to point to the Angels, saying: "Take heed that ye despise not one of these little ones; for I say unto you, That in heaven their angels do always behold the face of my Father which is in heaven " (St. Matt. xviii. 10). Ought Christ not rather to have said: "Fear God's anger"? And how can the Angels see or know our offences, while they behold always the face of their heavenly Father? Are they perhaps omniscient or omnipresent? I expect you will answer to the effect: "The Angels will know the offences through God anyhow." Now it is the same answer I give you with regard to the Saints. *How* they hear our prayers and supplications, our thanksgivings and praises, we do not know, but they will hear them through God anyhow. But a more serious question is started: "Why do you invoke the saints at all? Is it not sufficient to pray to God and Christ? Nay, is it not derogatory to his supreme honour, to seek a secondary help, as if he was either too austere a master, or changeable and more accessible to clever advocates?" My friend, you are sentenced by your own words, since you ask your brother here below to pray for you and with you. Or is the invocation of saints wrong because the saints have cast off sinfulness, whereas the Scripture allows you to ask the intercession of sinful men? But *the original cause and principal reason* of the Invocation of Saints is unknown to you, as you are ignorant of the true notion of both the Church and the Communion of Saints.

This chief reason is the "*Solidarité*" (alluded to above) which engages the individual members of the Church to each other, so that they may not and cannot be unconcerned at any loss or gain, joy or sorrow, activity or sloth of any member. If "one member suffer, all the members suffer with it, &c." "Likewise joy shall be in heaven over one sinner that repenteth, more than over ninety and nine just persons, which need no repentance" (St. Luke xv. 7).* This mutual engagement obliges the Church to work on towards the attainment of her great end, viz. God's glory and honour; that He may be all in all. The pilgrims here below assist each other on their way home. The saints above, although personally safe, having reached their happy home, do not, by merely changing places, discontinue their being partners in the Church-work. They encourage and push on the traveller by word and example, which they left behind them on their departure. They intercede incessantly for the success of the travellers, pleading before the throne of God, as a friend does in the case of his friend. Meanwhile we "Viatores debiles et lassi" stretch out our hands to the heavenly regions where good wishes for our welfare are entertained and prayers offered up by our friends and associates. However, both the "Viatores" here below, and the "Victores" there above feel a common sympathy for their faithful companions detained in the prison of Hades, both joining their efforts to release them. Thus the Church work goes on briskly below and above, every member co-operating with the others, on the grand plan

---

* You see they are better informed in heaven about our spiritual affairs than we may fancy. Protestantism is awfully anxious to keep heaven at a distance, and to deprecate its intermeddling with our affairs; but it is of no use denying or ignoring a bond which *de facto* exists, although you decline to reap its fruits and to avail yourselves of its blessings.

which Christ, the head of the members, laid down to God's honour and our eternal bliss. Thus this great *Co-operative Society* prospers *in* Christ, *with* Christ, and *through* Christ. Now, how is it possible to speak of dishonouring Christ by invoking his saints? Does not the whole turn on Christ, as the body on the soul, as the accidents on the substance? Is the Church not both χριστοφόρος (bearing Christ) and χριστόφορος (borne by Christ)? On the contrary, they dishonour Christ who deny this *co-operative* character of Christ's Church. In fact they quite misapprehend this efficacious Union of the triune Church, where no sound member ever dies or is severed from the others, no sound member remains solitary or destitute. Giving they receive, and receiving they give. Here you have the genuine type of Divine Socialism, aped and caricatured in the modern Phalanstères. St. Simon's reveries are but the abuse of a deep truth; and Lamennais transferred the qualities of the Catholic Church on the People universally.

Indeed it is rather unpleasant and tedious, after such a lofty aspect of the Communion of Saints, to review the frivolous objections of its opponents.— Mr. Archer Gurney, in a letter to the Editor of the "Union Chrétienne" (7 Jan. 1866), indulges in speculative fancymongery about the Catholic Church, intended to be what the Germans call "eine pragmatische Geschichtsauffassung," but what is in reality nothing but a novel visionary aspect of the Church, deprived of any objective basis. He says,

" qu'avec le temps une grande apostasie, c'est-à-dire *une grande corruption de la foi* se montrerait (as the Scriptures predict) au milieu de l'Église catholique, et elles (the Scriptures) nous en donnent trois marques distinctives... La seconde marque de la grande apostasie, c'est... le culte secondaire, tant des âmes des morts que des anges et des images." As to the great apostasy, it will certainly take place "au milieu de l'Église," but the Church *must and will* directly secrete the apostolical element which will be henceforward "hors de l'Eglise." A Church *tolerating Apostasy in her bosom!* is an idea which only a Protestant can conceive, who has ever so many new-fangled churches pullulating from the brains of those unshackled thinkers. Abbé Guettée very appositely remarks that the Church must preserve "le dépôt de la doctrine divine, et que tous ceux qui voudront posséder cette *vérité complète* devront s'unir à elle; nous croyons que cette Église ne peut exister qu' à la condition d'être *une réalité* et non une chimère, comme cette *Église idéale* que l'on a inventée en Occident, dans ces derniers temps, afin de pouvoir se persuader qu'on est dans l'Église chrétienne, même en n'y étant pas." With regard to the Invocation of Saints Mr. A. Gurney will allow us to give him some hints : 1st, to study a little more carefully the Bible, which plainly stigmatizes only the *pagan Hero-worship;* 2nd, not to swagger about the Fathers of the Church. St. Epiphanius speaks of the Antidicomarianites or Collyridiens who adored the Holy Virgin as a real *Goddess.* I very much doubt whether Mr. Archer Gurney read

the passage alluded to in the works of Epiphanius, at least he did not read it at full length (as he ought to have done), and if so, I leave it to the judgment of my readers, how anybody can *bond fide* advance Mr. A. Gurney's charge. Let him consult the Paris edition of St. Epiphanius (1622), p. 1003 : "Just as the perverse views of some heretics denying the Godhead of the Saviour, and severing him from the Father, drove others to the opposite error, and provoked them to say that the Father, the Son, and the Holy Ghost were one and the same person ; so the unworthy doctrines reflecting on the Virgin, drove some to the opposite extreme, and provoked to pay her *divine worship;* making her a *deity, offering cakes* (κολλύρια) in her name, and striving to honour her beyond due measure ; " p. 1064 : "God the Word ... clothed himself with flesh from the Holy Virgin ; but nevertheless not a virgin to be worshipped, nor that He might make her a *deity ;* not that we might *offer* in her name ; not that after so many generations women should become *priestesses.* ... Let Mary be in honour ; but let the Father, Son, and Holy Ghost be worshipped. Let no one *worship* Mary (τὴν Μαριὰμ μηδεὶς προςκυνείτω). ... These silly women offer to her the cake, or they take upon themselves to offer it in her behalf. The whole thing is foolish and strange, and is a device and deceit of the devil. .. Let Mary be in honour : let the Lord be worshipped (ὁ Κύριος προςκυνείσθω)."
À propos de "*cent* et *mille* citations (which Mr. A. Gurney says he could furnish) de Saint Irénée, de Saint Augustin, de Saint Ambroise, de Saint

Jean Chrysostome, d'Origène, de Tertullien et de bien d'autres qui affirment ou qui *semblent* (!) affirmer que *tout* culte appartient *exclusivement* à Dieu;" —I defy the learned gentleman to give me *one*, fancy, only *one*, passage of any Father of the Church against the Invocation of Saints, i.e. in proof of the unlawfulness of the Invocation of Saints.

This leads me to an observation I have made in reading books written by Anglo-Catholics. You will meet in the same with a tolerable amount of true Catholic teaching founded on the Fathers of the Church; but as the standard of the infallible Church is wanting, the amount varies according to the subjective disposition of the individual; so that also in the Anglo-Catholic denomination there is *no Unity of belief*, no more than in the rest of Protestantism. By "Unity of belief" I do not mean Unity in School Opinions, but Unity in dogmas (all of which the Church indispensably requires to hold), e. g. in the dogma of the Invocation of Saints. The Catholics are bound *necessitate fidei*, i. e. under penalty of forfeiting their eternal salvation, to hold *all* the dogmas (dogmata explicita sive declarata) without any difference, as among the dogmas *none are optional or adiaphorous.* Now the English Church, e. g. neither teaches nor enforces the dogma of the Invocation of Saints; and no Anglo-Catholic asserts more than that the English Church *cannot object to it:* CONSEQUENTLY in the English Church (even in the Anglo-Catholic sub-division) there is at least one dogma wanting, but the want of one destroys the Catholicity of the Church as much as the want

of all. *Therefore the Anglo-Catholics are*, MOST DE-
CIDEDLY, *no Catholics, but Protestants*, although Protestants inclining hopefully towards Catholicism.*
It is astonishing how the zealous Intercommunionists dive into the depths of Orthodox learning, rove
in the remotest districts, compile the minutest arguments, while they overlook *the chasm at their feet*.
They most ingenuously demand " de ne pas faire de
cérémonies," and to join hands all at once—to join
hands over *the vast deep* stretching out between
them!

But to return to our review, we find Mr. S. C.
Malan engaged in a controversy with Dr. Fraser
on the subject of Intercommunion between the
English and Orthodox Churches. In his words
there is no double dealing, no Jesuitical tortuous
ways, no childish wish of attaining the end without
employing the means, no anxious hastiness implying the fear of closer examination of this case,
which might cause the cherished idea to fall to the
ground. I like men of the stamp of Mr. Malan.
There is something attractive about such straight-

* We are desirous to hear what the Anglo-Catholics can reply to this my statement of *facts*. I do not expect to hear attempts to show the little importance of this dogma (the contrary to which I showed above), or the advisability of excluding its practical bearing—the only question on which my argument turns is the double unquestionable *fact*. 1. That the doctrine of the Invocation of Saints is, avowedly, a *dogma* of the Orthodox Church ; 2. That those who do not hold *all* the dogmas, are by the Orthodox Church considered not to belong to the Catholic Church.

forward and manly characters, and you like to deal with them. By the way, the Evangelical party has many such characters, and I ascribe chiefly to this circumstance the present vitality of that party.— Mr. Malan asks (Churchman, Sept. 28, 1865) Dr. Fraser one question : "When we talk of union with the Eastern Church, . . what is to be done about *the worship of the Virgin and of the Saints?* I have travelled extensively in the East—a better land than the West—and I have also spent a long time at Rome. . . . The result of my long experience is, that the Church of England is better than either the Greek or the Romish Church ; that the Greek comes next ; and that the Romish Church is unquestionably the worst of the three, but that as regards the worship of the Virgin and of the Saints, there is very little indeed to choose between the Eastern Church and that of Rome. This has prevented me from joining the Eastern Church Association, because I have too much experience not to be very matter-of-fact in such matters. *Two we know cannot walk together except they be agreed, and there can be no union without like feeling and like faith.* I have one Mediator between God and myself, and I want no more. The Virgin and the Saints are practically and to all intents and purposes additional Mediators for the members of the Greek and of the Romish Church. What, then, is to be done as to union in this case ? *Had we not better settle this first?* " Thus Mr. Malan declines the dogma of the Invocation of Saints on the ground of its being liable to be abused by popular superstitions. This fear of

Superstition lies at the bottom of the opposition. In fact, the doctrine of the Invocation of Saints is to one half of the English Church a *stumblingblock*, to the other a *bugbear*, but to none a *magnet* drawing towards the Church. What Mr. Malan says about the "additional mediators," is satisfactorily repelled by Dr. Fraser's reply to the above article (The Churchman, Oct. 12, 1865) : "Will not Mr. Malan admit that *a very decided sophism* lurks in the double meaning of the word 'Mediator'? Is not he himself a mediator, as well as every other Christian, whenever he says 'Forgive us our trespasses ?' If any Christian may be a mediator thus, it is *possible*—I say no more—that the Saints may also be so in the same way. No Greek, nor even Roman, Churchman would consider the Saints to be mediators in the mode in which our Saviour is 'our only mediator and advocate,' as partaking of the natures of both God and man, and so being a fit 'daysman' and intermediate between both." The reply is good, but Dr. Fraser, although a most decided Anglo-Catholic, cannot proceed beyond the '*possible.*' This plainly shows that the doctrine of the Invocation of Saints is *the sore place* of the English Church, the real *touchstone* of Catholicity. As soon as you touch upon this subject, you will find the Anglo-Catholic sensitive, reserved, timorous. *This is the reason why I thought it my duty to enlarge upon the matter beyond the due proportion of this pamphlet.* Dr. Fraser (and with him by far the greatest number of Anglo-Catholics) has not yet come to a clear understanding on the matter at issue. He openly confesses : "On the subject of the question which Mr. Malan addresses to me, I feel many difficulties. I hope that they may be solved as the desire for union increases; but I am not myself casuist enough to decide *at what point diversity of practice or of opinion should become a bar to unity.*" This is just the *signal mistake* of Dr. Fraser, that he considers the doctrine of the Invocation of Saints *an opinion* and not *a dogma.* The Orthodox Church is *most explicit* in this matter, much more than the Council of Trent. Has Dr. Fraser never consulted *Kimmel's Libri Symbolici Ecclesiæ Orientalis?* There he may read in the "Confessio Orthodoxa," p. 300, *seq.:* "Ἐπικαλούμεθα τὴν μεσιτείαν τῶν ἁγίων πρὸς Θεὸν, διὰ νὰ παρακαλοῦσι δι' ἡμᾶς. . . . Καὶ χρειαζόμεθα τὴν βοήθειάν τους, ὄχι ὡς ἂν νὰ μᾶς ἐβοηθοῦσαν ἐκεῖνοι ἀπὸ τὴν ἐδικήν τους δύναμιν· μὰ, διατὶ ζητοῦσιν εἰς ἡμᾶς τὴν χάριν τοῦ Θεοῦ μὲ ταῖς πρεσβείαις τους. . . . p. 304: Μάλιστα ἂν καταφρονήσωμεν τὴν μεσιτείαν τῶν ἁγίων, παροξύνομεν τὰ μέγιστα τὴν θείαν μεγαλειότητα, δὲν τιμῶντες τοὺς εἰλικρινῶς δουλεύσαντας αὐτῇ." "We implore the *Mediation* of the Saints with God, that they may intercede for us. . And we *need* their help, not as if they assisted us by their own power, but that they may apply in our behalf for grace of God through their prayers... *Yea, if we despise the mediation of the saints, we most grievously irritate the Divine Majesty*, not honouring those who unblamably served it (i. e. the Divine Majesty)." Moreover I refer to the acts of the Synodus Hierosolymitana, chiefly the VIIIth Decree (Ὅρος) of Dositheus, Patriarch of Jerusalem, and to the XVIIth

Chapter of the Confession of Metrophanes Critopulos. Remark in this Orthodox teaching the unequivocal decidedness and precision of language. What a gratifying contrast with the tame style and subdued voice of the Romish teaching in the Council of Trent, which seems to be made for entrapping converts, presenting the *minimum* and hiding the *maximum*. Let our course be the contrary, laying before the reader *the strongest language* of the Orthodox formularies, representing the practical working of the system. Can you heartily adopt this mode of thinking and living? If so, it is all right. If not, do not think of joining or constituting the Orthodox Catholic Church. It is nothing but a *hoax* of Orthodoxy. I saw the other day a strange little book, "Private Devotions as enjoined by the Holy Eastern Church, *for the use of her members.*" London, J. Masters, 1851. It is apparently the work of an Anglo-Catholic who took the trouble to clear the original of the stain of the Invocation of Saints, as the compiler ingenuously confesses in the Preface to the work: "We must also plead guilty to having, in one particular, adapted them (viz. the prayers) to English use, *by substituting*, wherever an invocation to the saints or to the blessed Virgin occurs, the words ' for Christ's sake,' or such like." If the compiler had intended the book for English Churchmen, we would have less to object, although also in this case he ought to have put on the title-page " revised and adapted to the use of English Churchmen;" but as he expressly writes "for the use of her members," i. e.

those of the Orthodox Church, I find the proceeding unjustifiable and downright Jesuitical. Is it not intended to *level*, in this insidious way, Orthodoxy with Anglicanism, in order to bring about a Union *on the ruins of Catholicity?*

But to proceed to the *strong language* of the Orthodox formularies, I choose a few pages of the " Εὐχολόγιον τὸ μέγα," Venice, 1862: p. 507, is said of the holy Virgin: "σὺ γὰρ εἶ ἡ σωτηρία τοῦ γένους τῶν χριστιανῶν,"—" for thou art the *salvation* of the Christian race." From p. 508—511 there occurs three times the "Theotokion:" "Παναγία Δέσποινα. . . παρακάλεσον, καὶ ἐλέησον ἡμᾶς." "Most holy Lady . . intercede (for us) and *have mercy on us.*" p. 519, of the holy Virgin: " Αὐτὸν (i. e. Θεὸν) ἐκδυςώπει ὑπὲρ πάντων ἡμῶν τοῦ κ. τ. λ." "*Induce* him for all of us to (send rain)." p. 520: " Πάντες μεσίτιν σε, . . . ἔχομεν." "All of us have you as our *Mediatrix*." On the same page she is called καταφύγιον στερρὸν καὶ ὅπλον ἄμαχον, " a strong refuge and unconquerable weapon." p. 521 : " Νενοσηκότας . . . τῇ εὐσπλαγχνίᾳ σου Δέσποινα θεραπεύσασα λύσον τῶν . . λυπηρῶν." "By thy compassion, O Lady, *heal and deliver* those who are sick from their sorrows." p. 535 : " Νεῦσον Ἀχραντε σωθῆναι τοὺς οἰκέτας σου." "*Annue*, Immaculata, *salvari* servos tuos." p. 544, the holy Virgin is called μόνη τῶν ἀνθρώπων βοήθεια, "*the only help* of man;" ἰαμάτων πηγή, "Sanationum fons." Further on: " . . πάντες σοι προςπίπτομεν (i. e. τῇ Παρθένῳ), τῇ κραταιᾷ σκέπῃ σου, Ἀγνὴ, σῶσον ἡμᾶς πάντας. . ." "We all *fall down* before thee (O Virgin); by thy mighty protection *save us all.*" p. 545 : Μαρία . . καθάρισον . ἡμᾶς, "Mary, *purify* us."—These passages will produce, I am sure, a most painful feeling on the sensitive nerves of Protestants, and will confound the Anglo-Catholics in the eyes of their Evangelical brethren, as they prided themselves to hold the same faith with the Orthodox. But I appeal to your common sense. If a man, destitute and unhappy to the utmost, approaches you, falls down, embraces your knees, conjuring you to help him, and, after you have helped him, calls you his only helper, should you consider this man a blasphemer, and his proceedings derogatory to God's honour? Neither you nor the man thought of interfering with the honour of God. You would say, all I approve that the man has said or done, for, *humanly speaking,* it is true and right. Why should we always expressly repeat that the *Mediation* of the Saints is only a secondary one? I think every one knows that by himself. St. Augustin *owes his eternal salvation* to his mother Monica, since she was the chief instrument, by which God operated on him. God *can and does* operate without intervening medium, as the case of St. Paul's conversion shows. But *the rule* is that God operates and dispenses His grace through the medium of His saints. The reason is obvious, as soon as you have well understood and weighed *the living and working triune Church.* Jesus Christ founded his Church to be a living and efficient Organism, which can only subsist by and through *mutual co-operation.* I showed above, how deeply

St. Paul understood and entered upon this vital characteristic of the Church. Now if the intercourse between the Triumphant and Militant Church were stopped, it would paralyse the whole Organism; in fact, it would destroy the same. Look round yourselves; does God not operate upon us through our fellow-members of the Church? Does He not dispense His grace chiefly by their hands? And still His arm is not shortened; He needs no assistant in his work. But to kindle faith, hope, and charity in the body of His Church, He appoints the members of His Church to be the channels of His grace to each other, in order to *cement the Church*, which is the mystical body of Christ.

Such a faint and dull shadow of the Church, as Dr. Fraser and the other Anglo-Catholics confess, cannot be very hopeful. I do not accede to Mr. Geo. Potessaro, who thinks, "if many Anglicans felt like him (Dr. Fraser), *the union of churches would soon be a reality*" (the Churchman, Sept. 28, 1865). I wish not to be misunderstood;. for personally I highly esteem both the character and zeal of Dr. Fraser. It is the same with Dr. Pusey, who has not the slightest idea of the *vital importance* of the dogma of the Invocation of Saints; otherwise he would not say: "I have on different occasions in public, and very often in private, *spoken against, discouraged, and prevented the use of any devotions except to God Alone*" (A letter to the Bishop of London, in explanation of some statements contained in a letter by the Rev. W. Dodsworth. Oxford, 1851,

p. 100).—Very poor indeed is Tract xc. on the matter. All it says is contained in the phrase: "Now there *was* a primitive doctrine on all these points (viz. Purgatory, Invocation of Saints, &c.), —how far Catholic or universal, is a farther question,—but still so widely received, and so respectably supported, that it may well be entertained *as a matter of opinion* by a theologian now" (p. 23).

The deepest and *conclusive* reason of the aversion to this doctrine, even with the most advanced Anglo-Catholics, is the *fear of superstition* which might attend the practice of this doctrine, and which *de facto* has attended it. However, in innumerable instances the indefatigable censurers grapple with shadows, awfully misinterpreting the respective passages, so awfully that it reminds me of Hamlet's words:

> Wise men know well enough,
> What monsters you make of them.

The right interpretation of most of the censured passages or expressions does not want a great amount of learning, but merely *common sense*. The same expression you find fault with as a divine, you use, perhaps, an hour later in every day life, unmindful of your own inconsistency. Still

> Fas est et ab hoste doceri.

And what do we learn then from the opposition of the Anglo-Catholics to this dogma? It shows clearly that their idea of the Church is defective and truly Protestant. In fact, the Anglo-Catholics assert scarcely more about our doctrine than the

Rationalistic Remonstrants did. Let us hear what *Phil. Limborch* (Theologia Christiana. Amsterdam, 1686, p. 476) says : " Potest quidem in precibus nostris mentio fieri Sanctorum, quibuscum Deus fœdus erexit, in cujus partem pii veniunt; ut nempe fœderis ac promissionum suarum meminisse velit. Ita olim Israëlitæ Deum precati sunt, ut memor fœderis cum Abrahamo, &c., erecti ipsis parcere velit: quoniam enim Deus respectu promissionis suæ parentibus factæ posteris gratiam facit, uti liquet 1 Reg. 15, 4, etiam promissionis illius in precibus mentio fieri potest. Sed ut per eorum merita a Deo exaudiri petamus, Deo plane injurium est. Et sive per merita sua Sancti intercedere dicantur, sive nobiscum orare tanquam sanctiores aut Deo conjunctiores, perinde est."

Since the fear of superstition will be the greatest difficulty to be overcome by English Churchmen, both in this point and on the whole in the work of Church union, let us add a few words

On Superstition.

Superstition is a prolific relic of the old serpent's poison. Although we are by Baptism cleansed from the Original Sin, the "fomes peccati" still remains. Every one of us has some inclination to superstition. But the more true religion, the less superstition, not (as people commonly fancy) the contrary. You may find

Atheists trembling for superstitious fear; and such a practical Atheist invented the verse:

> Timor fecit Deos.

It is very true what Disraeli said in the Sheldonian Theatre (25th November, 1864): "*Man is a being born to believe*, and if you do not come forward —if no *Church* comes forward, with all its title-deeds of truth sustained by the tradition of sacred ages, and the convictions of countless generations to guide him, *he will find altars and idols in his own heart and his own imagination.*" It is just the unbeliever who is practically most addicted to superstition, he who

> tremblant de faiblesse,
> Attend, pour croire en Dieu, que la fièvre le presse;
> Et, toujours dans l'orage au ciel levant les mains,
> Dès que l'air est calmé, rit des faibles humains.
> Car de penser alors qu'un Dieu tourne le monde,
> Et règle les ressorts de la machine ronde,
> Ou qu'il est une vie au-delà du trépas,
> C'est là, tout haut du moins, ce qu'il n'avoûra pas.

Why did, just in the last years, *Swedenborgianism* gain ground and attract the attention even of the higher classes of English Society? Swedenborgianism is but bare Unitarianism decked with some prophetic and mystic rags, a fine combination of unbelief and superstition. What do you say of *Spiritism*, Spirit rapping, Spirit correspondence, Table turning? Nil novi sub luna. A few years ago, when reading Tertullian's Apologeticus, I fell in with the following passage in the 23rd chapter (edit. Ritter. Elberfeld, 1828, p. 73): " Porro si et magi phantasmata edunt, et jam defunctorum infamant animas; si pueros in eloquium oraculi elidunt; si multa miracula circulatoriis præstigiis ludunt; si et somnia immittunt, habentes semel invitatorum angelorum et dæmonum assistentem sibi potestatem, per quos et capræ et *mensæ divinare* consueverunt: quanto magis, &c." From this one sees most clearly that the human heart yearns for communion with the other world, and if you preclude the lawful way of the Invocation of Saints and of the Prayers for the Departed, superstition will pour in through a hundred loop-holes. You think it better to abolish doctrines liable to superstitious abuses. Had you not better first remove Knife, Rope, and Sword, and empty the Ocean to prevent their ravages? Had we not better discard the Bible, which, torn from the body of the Church, creates heresy and schism? As long as Religion is conveyed in "earthen vessels" (2 Cor. iv. 7), faith will be mingled with superstition, wheat with tares, divine excellency with human frailty. Now the true Catholic Church may *never teach, nor support, nor tolerate Superstition*, but it is her province *always to oppose and combat it*. Döllinger (Kirche und Kirchen, p. xxxi.) expresses this thought masterly: "Auch das haben wir anzuerkennen, dass sich in der Kirche der Rost der Missbräuche, des abergläubischen Mechanismus, immer wieder ansetzt, dass die Diener der Kirche zuweilen durch Trägheit und Unverstand, das Volk durch Unwissenheit, das Geistige in der Religion vergröbern und dadurch erniedrigen, entstellen, zum eigenen Schaden anwenden. *Der rechte reformatorische Geist darf also in der Kirche nie entschwinden,* muss vielmehr periodisch mit neu verjüngender Kraft hervorbrechen, und in das Bewusstsein und den Willen des Klerus eindringen."

But to come nearer to the question, you point to Roman Catholicism and its superstitions fostered by the Popes and their votaries. Well, I have nothing to contradict; but *suffice it once for all to state, that Papism has apostatized from Catholic Orthodoxy, and has involved itself in Heresy and Schism.* Thus we have nothing to do with Papism, and consider it *not only a mistake but a blunder* of Dr. Pusey and of the large majority of Anglo-Catholics to long for a union with Rome. Let us not defile the pure Catholic deposit of faith, as preserved by the Orthodox Church, by shaking hands with Rome. NO TRUCE WITH PAPAL ROME! No compromise with Rome, before the Pope renounces his pretended Divine right, before he restores the pure Catholic faith and canons. The Romish tendencies within the Anglo-Catholic body are most pernicious to the development of this body. If mere aggrandizement is aimed at, you will do well to join Rome; but if the pure Catholic faith is your great mark, look to the rising sun: " *Ex Oriente lux !* " Does not Elijah's voice ring in your ears : " How long halt ye between two opinions ? if the Lord be God, follow him : but if Baal, then follow him. And the people answered him not a word." Either—or. *Will you be Romanists, then you can never be Orthodox Catholics.*

Are there superstitions to be found *in* the Orthodox Church? *Yes.* Are these superstitions *taught, supported, or tolerated by* the Orthodox Church? *No.* If you deny my statement, bring proofs to the contrary; but remember, all that *you* call superstition, is not therefore *real* superstition. Ponder my explanation given above, extracted from the writings of Orthodox authorities.

There is one Orthodox Church to which I wish chiefly to draw your attention, for two reasons: first, because its reputation is most undeservedly aspersed; secondly, because its prospects are bright, and its destiny great. I mean the *Russian Church.* Placed by Providence between the East and the West, it forms, as it were, the natural ligament of both. Not too proud to recognize and appropriate the scientific progress of the West, it is able to enter into the thoughts and feelings of the West. It knows and studies both Romanism and Protestantism. It knows and studies them, from choice and necessity, as it is, politically, in contact with both. It is eminently *the vital and formative (bildsam) element in the Eastern Church,* in contradistinction to other merely conservative bodies. *Within* the Russian Church there are superstitions, no doubt; but these are not superstitions *of* the Church, but *against* the Church. The Church continued to explode them, thus forming the "*Raskol*" (schism, heresy) *without* herself. Consult the Official Documents of the Raskol (Sbornik pravitelstvennych svedenii o Raskolnikach) compiled by Kelsieff, and you shall see how these sectarians are almost all mystical visionaries, grown in the native soil of superstition. The Church cut off those withered branches in order to preserve her own life, and by cutting them off showed her life and health unimpaired. The Russian Raskol is not to be compared with the English "Dissent." The Dissenters left the Church by their own accord; the Raskolniks were driven out by the authority of the Church. All shades of Dissent may openly remain in the Church; no Raskolnik may, and if he does, he can only do so surreptitiously and hypocritically. The Raskol is therefore the dark background, from which Orthodoxy sets off so much the brighter. The Dissent, on the contrary, is the living reproof of the deliquium of the English Church. Still there is one event which might seduce the superficial reader of Russian history into the belief that as early as 1551 the Russian Church sanctioned superstitious usages. I allude to the "*Stoglaff*" or the Council of the hundred chapters, held at Moscow under the 40th Metropolitan Macarius, of which A. N. Mouravieff (A History of the Church of Russia. Oxford, 1842, p. 104 and 105) relates: "Though the object of the Council itself was to eradicate superstitions and abuses; yet, notwithstanding all this, the prejudices and ignorance of the dark age of John showed themselves in some of the acts of this council, because there was no enlightened eye which could impartially overlook its decisions. . . . They did not apply to the œcumenical patriarchs to approve the Council of the Hundred Chapters. In this way it came to pass that certain superstitious customs and local errors were clothed with the sanction of authority, and taking root in time among the people, produced those pernicious schisms with which the Church is even yet afflicted. . . . . Its acts were *never confirmed* by the subscription of the Russian bishops; and not only has the original copy of them not been preserved, but none of the chronicles even so much as mention it, before the times of Nikon; and the metropolitan Macarius himself is silent concerning the council, in his Books of the Genealogies, in which he has related the history both of State and Church affairs." Since 1860 we possess the text of the Council published by Trübner, London [Stoglaff—Sobor byvshii v Moskve pri velikom gossudare tsarei velikom knäze Ivane Vassilyevitshe (v leto 7059)].

In finishing this first point we come to the conclusion that Anglo-Catholicism cannot lay claim to Catholic Orthodoxy; not only because it is part of a body composed of omnigenous Protestantism, but on the ground of its own *inherent* Protestantism. Let us conclude with a sweeping passage from Mr. Allies' work: " The Church of England Cleared from the Charge of Schism." Second Edition. Oxford, 1848, p. 506 *seq.* : " Farewell, indeed, to any true defence of the Church of

England, any hope of her being built up once more to an Apostolical beauty and glory, of recovering her lost discipline and intercommunion with Christendom, if she is by any act of her rulers, or any decree of her own, to be mixed up with the followers of Luther, Calvin, or Zwingle: with those who have neither love, nor unity, nor dogmatic truth, nor Sacraments, nor a visible Church among themselves: who, never consistent but in the depth of error, and the secret instinct of heresy, deny regeneration in Baptism, and the gift of the Holy Spirit in Confirmation and Orders, and the power of the keys in absolution, and the Lord's Body in the Eucharist. *That is the way of death;* who is so mad as to enter on it? When Protestantism lies throughout Europe and America a great disjointed mass, in all the putridity of dissolution,

Monstrum horrendum, informe, ingens, cui lumen, ademptum,

judicially blinded, so that it cannot perceive Christ dwelling in His Church, while she grows to the measure of the stature of the perfect man, and making her members and ministers His organs—who would think of joining to it a living Church? Have we gone through so much experience in vain? Have we seen it develop into Socinianism at Geneva, and utter unbelief in Germany, and a host of sects in England and America, whose name is Legion, and who seem to be agreed in nothing else but in the denial of sacramental grace and visible unity; and all this at the last hour, in the very turning point of our destiny, to seek alliance with those who have no other point of union but common resistance to the tabernacle of God among men? A persuasion that nothing short of the very existence of the Church of England is at stake, that one step into the wrong will fix her character and her prospects for ever, compels one to say that certain acts and tendencies of late have struck dismay into those who desire above all things to love and respect their spiritual mother. If the Jerusalem bishopric, the stillborn offspring of an illicit connection,

Cui non risere parentes,

be the commencement of a course of amalgamation with the Lutheran or Calvinistic heresy, who that values the authority of the ancient undivided Church will not feel his allegiance to our own branch of it *fearfully shaken?* 'May that measure utterly fail, and come to nought, and be as though it had never been.' *The time for silence is past. There is such a thing as 'propter vitam vivendi perdere causas.' It must be said publicly that such a course will lead infallibly to a schism, which will bury the Church of England in its ruins.* If she is to become a mere lurking-place for omnigenous latitudinarianism; if first principles of the Faith, such as baptismal regeneration, and priestly absolution, may be indifferently held or denied within her pale,—though, if not God's very truths, they are most fearful blasphemies,—THE SOONER SHE IS SWEPT AWAY THE BETTER." Thus far Mr. Allies. He is gone since; gone where we cannot follow him; gone where nobody expected him to go. Nobody did wonder at Dr. Newman joining the Romish Church. His propensity was, ever since he looked out for the Catholic Church, plainly Romish. He never looked to the East, never was kind to the East. But Mr. Allies studied the Eastern Church, loved it, defended it against the Romish pretensions. Why then is he gone where our eyes follow him sorrowing? Mr. Allies was a Western mind, born and trained in a Western atmosphere, imbued with Western notions. The Western mode of thinking, of feeling, of worshipping had pervaded, as it were, his system. He looked for the Catholic Church, i. e. that part which was in unison with his Western mind and heart, the Romish Church, which, in spite of her errors and innovations, is still the only exponent of Western Catholicism. *My dear Eastern friends, I conjure you not to undervalue the difference of the Eastern and the Western minds*, and their different forms of thinking and worshipping. The Roman-Catholic Church is wrong,—that is most true,—and she must be restored to Orthodox purity; otherwise she will not form a sound branch of the Universal Church; but it is a requisite of paramount importance, not to lose the Western ground, not to attempt to assimilate, extrinsically, the Eastern and Western Orthodox Churches. Both, though having the same faith and fundamental constitution of the Catholic Church, must keep their formal peculiarities, which have become a part of their innermost life, and which cannot be changed like a dress. Divine Providence framed the Western Church on the Western mind; therefore our Western form is *inalienable* from our Western minds.

Our difference from the East is only formal; but I venture to maintain that often *formal* obstacles were a more serious bar to unity than even *material* ones. Had the Orthodox Catholic Church of the West existed, Mr. Allies and thousands of seceders to Rome would have been fully satisfied, more than now, as they have to take Papacy with its ominous tail of consequences into the bargain. However, these Westerns prefer even the contaminated Western form to the pure Eastern, because the former is *congenial* to them.

II.

THE English Church claims *Apostolical Succession* for her bishops, and *valid Ordination* for her ministers. If both were granted, the sacramental character of the English Church would be settled, even if labouring under schism. There is a certain *correlativeness* between both, but it is rather negative and one-sided. By this I mean: a valid ordination *cannot* be made by an invalid bishop; it pre-supposes, therefore, Apostolical Succession. But a valid bishop *can* make an invalid ordination by not observing the proper "materia et forma sacramenti." It is not our mind to settle the historical question about the unbroken line of English Bishops.

Non nostrum est, tantas componere lites.

Within the pale of the English Church this seems

to be an undoubted fact. Beyond the English
Church both Catholics and Protestants find the
question considerably intricate, and so beset with
difficulties "that the orders are, to say the least,
exceedingly doubtful" (Milner's End of Controversy.
8th edition, p. 211).—We propose only to collect
some little stones lying in the way—"scrupulos
congerere"—and are anxious to know, how the
Anglicans will be able to clear them away.

The celebrated Hooker was an eminent Anglican divine, "perhaps the most profound and accurate amongst them" (Milner, l. c. p. 208). He
says: "There may be sometimes very just and
sufficient reason *to allow ordination made without a
bishop.* Where the Church must needs have some
ordained, and neither hath nor can have possibly a
bishop to ordain, in case of such necessity the ordinary institution of God hath given *oftentimes*, and
may give place. And therefore *we are not simply
without exception to urge a lineal descent of power from
the Apostles by continued succession of bishops in every
effectual ordination.*" (Quoted by Macaulay in his
Review of Gladstone's "On Church and State."
London, 1851, p. 50.) Have you ever heard anything more *un-Catholic?* Fancy one of these priests
not ordained by a bishop, and therefore (on Catholic principles) mere laymen, elevated to the rank
of a bishop, and ordaining priests! Would one
such lay-bishop not break through the Apostolical
line of bishops and annihilate the claim of Apostolical Succession?

"Hundreds, both in King Edward's and in

Queen Elizabeth's reign, ministered in the Church of England as legal pastors, *who had no episcopal ordination*" (Protestant Ordinations examined by the Rev. H. Smith. London. p. 48). Hooker (Eccl. Pol. Book VII. p. 285) says: "The whole Church visible being the true original subject of all power, it hath not ordinarily allowed any other than bishops alone to ordain: howbeit, as the ordinary course in all things is ordinarily to be observed, *so it may be in some cases necessary that we decline from the ordinary ways.*"—Hooker (Eccl. Pol. VI. 8): "Let the bishops continually bear in mind, that it is *rather the force of custom*, whereby the Church, having so long found it good to continue under the regimen of her virtuous bishops, doth still uphold, maintain, and honour them in that respect, than that any such true and heavenly law can be showed, by the evidence whereof it may of a truth appear, that the Lord himself hath appointed presbyters for ever to be under the regimen of bishops. *Their authority is a sword, which the Church hath power to take from them.*" On Hooker's views, Warburton, a no less learned divine, remarks, "The great Hooker was not only against, but laid down principles that have *entirely subverted* all pretences to a divine, unalterable right in any form of Church government whatever."—Bishop Cosins, who, upon the continent of Europe, *took the Lord's Supper* repeatedly in Presbyterian Churches, says, "Are all the Churches of Denmark, Sweden, Poland, Germany, France, Scotland, in all points, either of substance or circumstance, disciplinated alike?

Nay, they neither are, nor can be; nor yet need be, since it cannot be proved that any set and exact particular form is recommended to us by the word of God" (Ans. to Abstr. sect. 18, p. 58).—Field says: "Who, then, dare condemn all those worthy ministers of God, *who were ordained by Presbyters* in sundry Churches, at such times as bishops, in those parts where they lived, opposed themselves against the truth of God?" (Book III. c. 37.) Francis Mason, an enthusiastic defender of the Anglican Church, says: "If you mean by Divine right, that which is according to Scripture, then the pre-eminence of bishops is *jure divino*. . . . But if by *jure divino* you understand a law or commandment of God binding all Christian Churches perpetually, unchangeably, and with such absolute necessity that no other order of regimen may in any case be admitted, *in this sense neither may we grant it, nor yet can you prove it to be jure divino.*" The same Mason says (Def. of Foreign Ord. Oxford, 1641, p. 160): "Seeing a Presbyter is equal to a Bishop in the power of order, *he has equally intrinsical power to give orders.*"—Stillingfleet (Irenicum, p. 10) says: "I doubt not but to make it evident, that before these late unhappy times, the main ground for settling episcopal government in this nation, *was not any pretence* of Divine right, but the conveniency of that form to the state and condition of this Church at the times of its reformation."—Bishop Hall, who is found in Dr. Pusey's Catena, says: "Blessed be God, *there is no difference in any essential matter betwixt the Church of England and her sisters of the Re-*

formation. We accord in every point of Christian doctrine, without the least variation. Their public confessions and ours are sufficient convictions to the world of our full and absolute agreement. The only difference is in the form of outward administration, wherein also we are so far agreed, as that *we all* profess this form *not to be essential* to the being of a Church" (Peacemaker, sect. 6). We should feel greatly indebted to Dr. Pusey if he would give us a *Catholic interpretation* of such a *specifically Protestant* passage of one of the most prominent Anglo-Catholic Doctors of the Church!!—Archbishop Bramhall (Works, fol. 164) writes of the Presbyterian Churches: "Do I ... account them formal schismatics? No such thing. *It is not at all material,* whether episcopacy and priesthood be two distinct orders or distinct degrees of the same order."—Archbishop Usher writes : " For the testifying of my communion with these Churches, which I do love and honour *as true members* of the Church universal, I do profess *that with like affection I would receive the blessed sacrament at the hands of the Dutch* (i. e. presbyterial) *ministers in Holland, as I would do at the hands of the French ministers.*"—Archbishop Wake (the same who transacted with Du Pin, under sanction of Cardinal de Noailles, on the Intercommunion between the Romish and English Churches) writes : " I should be *unwilling to affirm,* that where the ministry is not episcopal, there is no Church nor any true administration of the sacraments; and *very many* there are among us, who, zealous for episcopacy, yet *dare not go so far as to annul* the ordinances of God performed by any other ministry."

The last twelve passages are quoted by Dr Cumming in his "Lectures on Tractarianism and Popery," Third Edition. London. p. 58—61. I need not add that I consider those lectures to be nothing but "*geistreicher Flugsand,*" interspersed with such startling "inventions and discoveries" that the author ought to take out a patent for the same. Thus he has found out that " Cain was, in principle, the first Roman Catholic priest; and Abel, in principle, was the first Protestant martyr" (p. 29). Still the quotations (as far as reliable) are useful materials for better purposes. Here we may collect from the same:

1. That the "Anglo-Catholic Fathers" were, on the point of Apostolical Succession and its needfulness, not so strict as Dr. Pusey and the modern Anglo-Catholics, but held rather Latitudinarian views subversive of the whole fabric of the Church;

2. That the boasted *Unity and Concord* of Anglo-Catholicism, even in *essentials* (to which the Hierarchy belongs agreeably to Catholic teaching), is a *specious illusion;*

3. That Anglo-Catholicism is *genuine Protestantism* decked and disfigured by Catholic spoils.

The Catholic Church never recognized ordinations made by presbyters. It is notorious that, when the Arians charged St. Athanasius with having ill-treated the priest Ischyras, the synod of Alexandria declined this charge on the score of

Ischyras not being a priest, *because he had not been ordained by a bishop*, but by the schismatic priest Colluthus, who had ordained many, all of whom the Church considered mere laymen.

Hooker's *exception* would destroy the whole fabric of an Apostolic Church. But what Hooker made an exception, Archbishop Cranmer and Bishop Barlow made a *rule*. For they answered to the question:

"Whether in the New Testament be required any consecration of a bishop and priest, or only appointing to the office be sufficient?"

Cranmer. In the New Testament, he that is appointed to be a bishop, or a priest, *needeth no consecration* by the Scripture, for election or appointing thereto is *sufficient*.

Barlow. That *only* the appointing is necessary. Macaulay therefore concludes justly (l. c. p. 52): "We do not pretend to know to what precise extent the canonists of Oxford agree with those of Rome as to the circumstances which nullify orders. We will not, therefore, go so far as Chillingworth. We only say that we see *no satisfactory proof of the fact that the Church of England possesses the apostolical succession.*"

"There is the same necessity of an apostolical succession of *mission*, or authority, to execute the functions of holy orders, as there is of the holy orders themselves. . . . Conformably to this, Dr. Berkley (in his sermon at the consecration of

Bishop Horne) teaches, that 'a defect in the *mission* of the ministry *invalidates* the sacraments, affects the purity of public worship, and therefore deserves to be investigated by every sincere Christian'" (Milner, l. c. p. 213). Now Dr. Berkley cannot have considered this Mission as being *implied* in the consecration as modern Anglicans use to do, who feel the difficulty of deriving the *Apostolical* Mission from the *State*. And still it is so. "Authority of jurisdiction, *spiritual* and temporal," says the statute of 1 Edward VI. c. 2, "is derived and deducted from the king's majesty, *as supreme head of these churches and realms of England and Ireland.*" Elizabeth undertook to place Matthew Parker in the See of Canterbury, "*supplying, by her supreme authority,*" any defects or impediments to his ordination,* and then declaring it *valid* by the agency of her obsequious parliament. In him she laid the foundation of a new fabric, which she herself modelled and constructed, "the church by law established," which subsists to this day (Kenrick : The Primacy of the Apostolic See. 3rd Edition, London, 1849, p. 266).

The consecration of Matthew Parker was invalid because the *forma sacramenti* was *insufficient*. This *forma*, or the words used in conferring the episcopal dignity, were :

* Parker was never considered by the Catholics to be a bishop. Even Le Courayer admits of this : "Il est constant que sous Elisabeth les catholiques anglais refusèrent de reconnaître Parker pour évêque, aussi bien que ceux qu'il avait consacrés : Sanderus, Stapleton, Harding, et tous ceux qui ont écrit contre les anglais, en fournissent des preuves authentiques."

"Take the Hollie Gost, and remember that thou stirre upp the grace of God, which is in the, by the imposicion of handes, for God hath not given us the Spirite of fear, but of Power, and love and soberness." *

This form might be used with just as much propriety in Confirmation, since we find in it not *the slightest allusion* to the sacrament of order. Now I apply, not to a deep canonical learning, but to *plain common sense,* if it is not unheard of to confer an office without even mentioning it ? The Anglicans themselves felt this want, and introduced in 1662 the still existing form: " Receive the Holy Ghost for *the office and work of a Bishop in the Church of God now committed unto thee by the imposition of our hands,* &c." This alteration is not so insignificant as the Anglicans would like to make us believe, but it is an alteration of *the utmost importance.* For *slight* reasons fixed religious forms are not altered. But they discovered a *flaw* in the form of consecration and tried to *repair* it; but, unfortunately, the pre-

---

* Dr. Pusey (Eiren. p. 232, *seq.*) seems to intimate that this form was the same or similar to that used in the consecration of Archbishop Chichele ("It has indeed escaped observation, that the form adopted at the consecration of Archbishop Parker was *carefully framed on the old form* used in the consecration of Archbishop Chichele, a century before—as I found by collation of the Registers in the Archiepiscopal Library at Lambeth, now many years ago—"). We should feel extremely obliged to Dr. Pusey, if he would tell us the exact wording of Chichele's consecration, i. e. the form said to be identical or equivalent to that used with Parker. If both forms proved to be the same (which I very much doubt), the consequence would be that Chichele's consecration was *simply null.*

ceding consecration of bishops could not be made valid by the later improved form. Had Parker been consecrated conformably to the present form the case would lie quite differently. But as Parker's consecration was invalid, the Apostolic line was broken off, irremediably broken off. The Anglican difficulty lies, if not solely, at least *chiefly* in the *deficient form* of Episcopal Consecration. Perrone (Prælectiones theologicæ. Paris, 1842, tom. I. p. 484, *seq.*) says : " Quodsi invalidæ censentur ordinationes Anglicanæ, non ideo est, quia ab episcopis hæreticis et schismaticis conferuntur, sed tum ob defectum successionis episcoporum, tum *ob vitiatam essentialiter formam.*" Liebermann (Institutiones theologicæ. Moguntiæ, 1861. Editio nona, tom. II. p. 731) says : " Præcipuum controversiæ pondus *in quæstione juris* est. Certum est, Parkerum a Barlowio ordinatum fuisse juxta formam ritualis ab Eduardo VI. editi. Videndum igitur est, an hic ritus ea habeat quæ ad substantiam sacramenti pertinent. Imprimis de *forma* ordinationis quæstio instituitur." Dr. F. G. A. Grosch (Grundzüge des Kirchenrechtes der Katholiken und Evangelischen. Breslau, 1845, p. 148, note): "Nur die Weihe, welche von einem ausserhalb der Kirche zugleich aber in ununterbrochener Succession von den Aposteln stehenden Bischofe in dem vorgeschriebenen Ritus ertheilt worden ist, erkennt die Kirche als gültig (valida) an. Daher sind die Weihen der griechischen Bischöfe gültig, dagegen die der englischen Bischöfe, *welche bei Ertheilung der Weihen von den ursprünglichen Förmlichkeiten abgewichen sind, ebenso un-*

gültig, resp. nichtig, wie die der dänischen und schwedischen Bischöfe, deren Succession unterbrochen ist."

In order to obviate the objection, which might be made, that the authorities cited above are Roman-Catholic: I beg to remark that the Roman-Catholic doctrine of the sacrament of order, and the practice based thereon, are *perfectly Orthodox;* and Rome never disagreed in this point with the East. *True Episcopacy and sacramental operation* in both churches form the mysterious bond, in spite of strife and antagonism. Rome, although degenerated from what it was in happier times, when the East and the West were still undivided, when the Bishop of Rome held still the Primacy without affecting the Supremacy—Rome, I say, is and ever will be *infinitely nearer and dearer to the heart of the East, and the East to the heart of Rome*, than Protestantism ever can be. We rejoice at the traces of Orthodoxy which are still left in the Church of Rome, and consider them the stepping-stones which mark the way back to the primitive purity which the East so providentially preserved. Far from us the wild cry: " Rather Protestant than Papist! " Certainly, *neither of the two*, but least of all Protestant.

Rome's dealing with the Anglican clergy who went over to her, is a true pattern of Orthodox dealing. If Rome considered all ordinations by Parker and his successors, i. e. the whole present English Episcopate and Clergy, to be invalid, null and void, and, consistently, *re-ordained* * all those converts

---

* Liebermann (Institutiones theologicæ, Tom. II. p. 370) says: " Neque illud omittendum, quod potuerint ad ecclesiam accedere, qui

who wished and were fit for orders: the Eastern Church can but imitate her proceedings, as both follow, in this point, the very same principles. Yea, it is noticeable that Rome, though in many respects guilty of the Jesuitical bias of eager Proselytism, yet, in this point, continued *rigorously Orthodox*. Rome's recognition of Anglican orders would have been a successful *bait* to allure English clergymen into her communion. But she resisted firmly the temptation, and, by her practice, cut off for ever *the remotest thought or faintest hope* of yielding to the contrary. This *Impossibility* of yielding Dr. Newman seems not to be quite prepared to affirm, but I fear his opinion stands very *solitary*, and will create uneasiness and dissatisfaction among his co-religionists. *The fact of " reordination" is the final and conclusive verdict on the Invalidity of Anglican Ordinations.* By this *fact* all further controversy is broken off and indisputably settled.

Finally, I cannot refrain from quoting the admirable passage from Froude's History of England (London, 1863, tom. VII. p. 174): " A Catholic bishop holds his office by a tenure untouched by the accidents of time. Dynasties may change — nations may lose their liberties—the firm fabric of

se dicebant ab episcopis hæreticis ordinatos, de quibus an characterem episcopalem habuerint non constabat; quippe fortassis se ipsos multitudinis tumultuantis impetu intruserunt. Aut incertum erat, an legitima forma aut cum debita materia administratum fuerit sacramentum. Ejusmodi ordinationes dubiæ iterabantur, *et quidem sine conditione:* id enim per mille et ducentos annos in usu ecclesiæ non erat ut conditio adjiceretur."

society itself may be swept away in the torrent of revolution—the Catholic prelate remains at his post; when he dies, another takes his place; and when the waters sink again into their beds, the quiet figure is seen standing where it stood before—the person perhaps changed—the thing itself rooted like a rock on the adamantine basements of the world. The Anglican hierarchy, far unlike its rival, was a child of convulsion and compromise: it drew its life from Elizabeth's throne, and *had Elizabeth's throne fallen, it would have crumbled into sand.* The Church of England was as a limb *lopped off from the Catholic trunk;* it was cut away from the stream by which its vascular system had been fed; and the life of it, as an independent and corporate existence, *was gone for ever.* But it had been taken up and *grafted upon the State.* If not what it had been, it could retain the *form* of what it had been—the form which made it respectable, without the power which made it dangerous. The image, in its outward aspect, could be made to correspond with the parent tree; and to sustain *the illusion,* it was necessary to provide bishops who could appear to have inherited their powers by the approved method as successors of the apostles."

INTERCOMMUNION

is the great word echoed from certain quarters of the English Church, hailed by fervent believers and devout souls. It is a watchword, implying the joy of expectation and the power of pressing forward—but, alas! implying in the same time *the sad want of the thing longed for*, the melancholy consciousness of an ill-omened deficiency. The *Insulation* of the English Church, which is not recognized by *any* Catholic Church, may escape the observation of those Churchmen,

Qui reposaient la nuit et dormaient tout le jour;

but weighs heavily upon the minds of those who look beyond the average distance. Intercommunion is but another word for *Unity restored;* and Unity is one of the characteristics of the Catholic Church. There is no Unity in the Church without Intercommunion of the Churches. The "*invisible Unity*" is the poorest expletive of *Theology in a fix.* Unity refers to doctrine and to the fundamental constitution of the Church. Two Churches may disagree in discipline (e. g. the paschal controversy) without loosening the bond of Unity. Two Churches *never* may disagree in dogmas, as the English Church opposed to the Catholic Church does. Or is our above-made statement, based on the acknowledged doctrine of the Orthodox Church, and substantiated by passages from her Church-books, an illusion? No, there is no tergiversation; *you may not hold the complete Orthodox doctrine, as long as you remain in the English Church;* and if you do so, you are no upright Churchmen, you are Anglican hypocrites. Dr. Pusey does *not* hold the complete Catholic doctrine, and " we are glad that Dr. Pusey has spoken out his full mind; and we sincerely hope that no one will in future suppose him to be a whit less Protestant or more Catholic in opinion than he has now declared himself to be" ("The Month," December, 1865, p. 621). The Evangelicals and the Broad-Churchmen will understand me and fully appreciate my words, while they will condemn the Orthodox Church as unscriptural or un-protestant. Their condemnation is consistent with their views; and consistency I like as much as I detest disingenuous manipulation. Why do you wish for a forbidden fruit? Do you perhaps think, Orthodoxy would enter into a compromise with Anglicanism, throwing overboard the treasures she has jealously watched and kept for eighteen centuries past? Let us for a moment grant what is impossible, viz. that the Orthodox Church sacrificed half the lot of disagreeing doctrines, and requested you to adopt the other half. What would you do? Convocation is impotent and incompetent to settle doctrines. Parliament is unwilling to heighten the standard of belief; or would defer the matter "ad Calendas Græcas;" or would enjoin a *Creed by Act of Parliament!* Thus no hope is left, but sheer despair!

However, to illustrate the matter more distinctly, I will put a few questions.

" Shall Intercommunion be established between the English Church, *taken as a whole*, and the Orthodox Church?"

But there is *no Unity* within the English Church. The intestine divisions split her into as many Churches. The English Church is nothing but a conventional name for an aggregate of disparate components *bound together solely by the same roof and food.* "Mr Gladstone dwells much on the importance of unity in doctrine. Unity, he tells us, is essential to truth. And this is most unquestionable. But when he goes on to tell us that this unity is the characteristic of the Church of England, that she is one in body and in Spirit, we are compelled to differ from him widely. The apostolical succession she may or may not have. But *Unity she most certainly has not, and never has had.* It is matter of perfect notoriety, that her formularies are framed in such a manner as to admit to her highest offices men who differ from each other more widely than a very high Churchman differs from a Catholic, or a very low Churchman from a Presbyterian; and that the general leaning of the Church, with respect to some important questions, has been sometimes one way and sometimes another. Take, for example, the questions agitated between the Calvinists and the Arminians. Do we find in the Church of England, with respect to those questions, that unity which is essential to truth? Was it ever found in the Church? Is it not certain that, at the end of the sixteenth century, the rulers of the Church held doctrines as Calvinistic as ever were held by any Cameronian, and not only held them, but persecuted everybody who did not hold them? And is it not equally certain, that the rulers of the Church have, in very recent times, considered Calvinism as a disqualification for high preferment, if not for holy orders? Look at the questions which Archbishop Whitgift propounded to Barret, questions framed in the very spirit of William Huntingdon, S. S.* And then look at the eighty-seven questions which Bishop Marsh, within our own memory, propounded to candidates for ordination. We should be loth to say that either of these celebrated prelates had intruded himself into a Church whose doctrines he abhorred, and that he deserved to be stripped of his gown. Yet it is quite certain that one or other of them must have been very greatly in error. John Wesley again, and Cowper's friend, John Newton, were both Presbyters of this Church. Both were men of ability. Both we believe to have been men of rigid integrity, men who would not have subscribed a Confession of Faith which they disbelieved for the richest bishopric in the empire. Yet, on the subject of predestination, Newton was strongly attached to doctrines which Wesley designated as "blasphemy, which might make the ears of a Christian to tingle." Indeed, it will not be disputed that the clergy of the Established Church are divided as to these questions, and that her formularies are not found practically to exclude even scrupulously honest men of both sides from her altars. *It is notorious that some of her most distinguished rulers think this latitude a good thing, and would be sorry to see it restricted in favour of either opinion.*† . . . . But what becomes of the unity of

---

* "One question was, whether God had from eternity reprobated certain persons; and why? The answer which contented the Archbishop was "Affirmativè, et quia voluit."

† Only a few days ago (on the 13th February, 1866) the actual

the Church, and of that truth to which unity is essential? .... Is it not mere mockery to attach so much importance to unity in form and name, *where there is so little in substance,* to shudder at the thought of two Churches in alliance with one State, and to endure with patience the spectacle of *a hundred sects battling within one Church?* .... He (Mr. Gladstone) objects to the vote for Maynooth, because it is monstrous to pay one man to teach truth, and another to denounce that truth as falsehood. But it is a mere chance whether any sum which he votes for the English Church in any colony will go to the maintenance of an Arminian or a Calvinist, of a man like Mr. Froude, or of a man like Dr. Arnold. It is a mere chance, therefore, whether it will go to support a teacher of truth, or one who will denounce that truth as falsehood" (Macaulay on Gladstone, l. c. p. 53—57). No wonder that Dr. Pusey has strong misgivings on the want of unity in the Church. He says (A letter to the Bishop of London, 2nd Edition, Oxford, 1851, p. 188 *seq.*) : " Again, we must admit, *all upon all sides cry out, that there should not be this conflicting teaching.* While some of us are anxious to come to a better understanding with one an-

Archbishop of Canterbury replied to a deputation, headed by Lord Ebury, on the Revision of the Liturgy : " Each school of thought has, since the days of the Reformation, found a resting-place within the pale of the Church of England. She has been a loving mother to us all. May we still continue to repose together in her bosom and cultivate that Spirit of peace and good-will which is quite consistent with the earnest convictions of a different stamp on either side."

other, others are anxious to cast out those who differ from them. The great outcry which is ringing through our great towns (although in great degree arising from those external to the Church), yet, as far as it comes from Churchmen, is an *acknowledgment that the state of things is not right, that there ought not to be so many various voices.* Multitudes will, I trust, abide patiently, trusting that when this Babel-cry is *past* (?!) the Church will be allowed, in peace within and without, and seeking the peace of her children, to bring them to a right understanding with one another. But now, it does press hardly upon some who would serve the Church devotedly, whether this clamour be not perhaps the voice of the Church, whether both parties who speak against one another, do really at all misunderstand one another, *or whether they can ever be brought to understand one another in the one truth.*"

But the deficiency of Unity Dr. Pusey tries to compensate by showing the Life pervading the English Church (Eiren. p. 276 *seq.*). Now as real *Life* presupposes *Truth*, and truth presupposes *Unity*, he thinks to return more safely to his end. By this Dr. Pusey transfers the matter on a dangerous ground; for who is to decide whether the pretended Life is *real organic Life*, or a mere *Counterfeit of Life?* If you commit the judgment to the spectators, the sentences will be contradicting. If Dr. Pusey is the spectator, he will, of course, easily find out the Life which he is anxious to discover in the Church. This "something which is going on in the Church" a Broad-Churchman might term a "strong party feeling," a "spirit of cast," "ceremonizing, drilling, trimming, &c.," but he never will discover "healthy life." No more will the Evangelical, who pities the High-Churchman for fixing his eyes on trifles, while losing sight of the "One thing necessary." This "stirring and moving" in the Church is certainly derived from "individual life" in members of the Church, not, however, from the English Church itself, *which is devoid of priesthood and sacraments.* It is Queen Elizabeth who brought in this new-fangled priesthood, when the old Protestant episcopate was nearly extinct. Only five of Edward's bishops were left, of whom Kitchen's "character did not bear inspection," and Bale was "a foul-mouthed ruffian," and Barlow's consecration was attested by a "blank in the episcopal registers."—" Her (Elizabeth's) own creed was a perplexity to herself and to the world. With no tinge of the meaner forms of superstition, she clung to practices which exasperated the Reformers, while the Catholics laughed at their inconsistency; her crucifixes and candles, if adopted partly from a politic motive of conciliation, were in part also an expression of that half-belief with which she regarded the symbols of the faith; and while ruling the clergy with a rod of iron, and refusing as sternly as her father to tolerate their pretensions to independence, she desired to force upon them a special and semi-mysterious character; to dress them up as counterfeits of the Catholic hierarchy; and half in reverence, half in contempt, compel them *to assume the name and charac-*

ter *of a priesthood which both she and they in their heart of hearts knew to be an illusion and a dream*" (Froude). It is a mystical dream of Dr. Pusey, if he thinks to perceive the sacramental working and the vigorous life of the English Church—βίος ἀβίωτος (a life wanting the very requisites of sound life), nothing else. Such a subjective fancy cannot be dispelled by any argument, no more than the vagaries of any other mystical sect. I have witnessed Irvingite life, and Mormon life, and was (though a mere looker-on), by over-exertion, almost frightened into the beneficial silent death of Quakerism. "Some have all along been in the habit of looking to certain modes of revival; at the best, to the way in which God blessed the workings of one class of individuals. To these they appealed, as furnishing 'tokens of life in the English Church.' For myself, I always turned away, sick at heart, from this feverish *watching for tokens of life*. It is not in the flush of the cheek or the more brilliant eye alone, in which you would recognize the returning health of the body. These might be fever, not health-tokens. What is concentrated around individuals, even though manifoldly multiplied, is individual still. *To us, the workings seemed* all along far beyond any efforts of human zeal or energy or faithfulness, even as blessed by God" (Pusey, Eiren. p. 279 *seq.*). *To others*, the workings of the English Church seemed *not* to be beyond individual agency —καρποὶ τοῦ λόγου τοῦ σπερματικοῦ. What Dr. Pusey observes on the life in the English Church, is his personal opinion, is a debatable ground, and consequently of no use in establishing great principles.

Still in order to show more fully how the very same thing presents two extremely different aspects according to where you take your stand, either here on the rock of the Church or yonder on the drifting sand of Churchism—I select, for dissection, the "locus palmaris" (Pusey, Eiren. p. 276 *seq.*), putting in brackets [ ] the Catholic view of the matter. "Those who have pointed to 'life' as a great note in the English Church, did not mean the life of grace in individuals. They have meant the organic operation of God the Holy Ghost upon the Church *as a whole*. [Did ever the English Church act *as a whole*? When did it step forward as *one* body? Never. How, then, can Dr. Pusey show the pretended operation upon the Church as a whole? At the best, it is only an individual quickening on a larger scale than at other more different times.] It is the mark given by our Lord Himself. By a wonderful analogy between nature and grace, the branch, which had been severed from the True Vine, carried out with it for a time the life of the tree; but, the life-giving sap being cut off, after a time it withered. [Very true. But how long the period extends till withering becomes death, God alone knows. The Arians, Nestorians, Monophysites are not yet dead—why should Anglicanism, which is a thousand years younger, already be dead? Nay, it may (like the Lutheranism of the last thirty years) by some superior genius be galvanized into a kind of high life. Let us, therefore, wait a while longer and watch the symptoms of decay, the stages of the withering going on steadily. It is of no use growing impatient on account of history rolling on slowly. But, likewise, it is of no use building sanguine hopes and gratuitous assertions on the fact that the Church, which will break down to-morrow, has not yet broken down to-day.] Contrariwise, as our friend observed ("Catholicity of the English Church," in British Critic, No. LIII. p. 77), the Church of England has had a *tough, vigorous life.* [Because it was "*grafted upon the State ;*" and "had Elizabeth fallen, it would have crumbled into sand." Macaulay (Gladstone, p. 69) remarks very appositely: " We should say that the State which allied itself with such a Church postponed the primary end of government to the secondary : and that the consequences had been such as any sagacious observer would have predicted. Neither the primary nor the secondary end is attained. The temporal and spiritual interests of the people suffer alike. *The minds of men, instead of being drawn to the Church, are alienated from the State.*" This is the *tough, vigorous life. Tough* it was, because it was the life of a society "established by law," and this Establishment formed part of the "English Constitution." But *vigorous* it, most decidedly, was *not*, as the Church underwent all the great vicissitudes to which State-institutions are liable. It is true, Dr. Pusey declines to recognize that the Church drew its life from the State, and points to the "American *Protestant* Episcopal Church." But

CATHOLIC ORTHODOXY. 83

beware! If you are in communion with a *Protestant* Church, your Catholic claims are forfeited. You allude to its present flourishing state; but we know the up-and-downs of heresy. There is always some sect *en vogue*. So it was with Baptism; so it is now with Unitarianism. Of course American Anglicanism is more uniform than the English Establishment, since it has no attractive endowments, no support from the State. Broad and Low Churchmen are, therefore, at liberty to associate with any other more congenial denomination. Nevertheless there is no true Catholic decisiveness in the American Church, but pale and sickly irresolution, the ominous bequest of the English mother-church. Read but a few numbers of the "American Church Review," and your eyes will be opened on the pretended life of the American Church. It is perhaps not so insignificant, not so despicable as some other sects, but, after all, it is merely a *fashionable Protestant sect* — nothing else.] Its life has been tried in every way in which it could be tried. "It has been practised upon by theorists, browbeaten by sophists, [successfully] intimidated by princes, betrayed by false sons, [which means, in many cases, denounced as a human fabric by those who left her for conscience's sake,] laid waste by tyranny, [as well as it was planted and fostered by tyranny,] corrupted by wealth, torn by schism, and persecuted by fanaticism [—and it remained unshaken and invariable?! Oh no; intimidation, treachery, tyranny, corruption, persecution shook the fabric effectually, and proved that it was not built on a rock!] Revolutions have come upon it sharply and suddenly to and fro, hot and cold, as if to try what it was made of [—and they found they could make of it what they liked. Henry, Edward, Mary, Elizabeth, all saw their parliaments equally obsequious, changing Articles of religion like dresses.] It has been a sort of battle-field, [where heresy was uppermost,] on which opposite principles have been tried [and the heterodox was victorious.] No opinion [and dogma!], however extreme any way, but may be found, as the Romanists are not slow to reproach us, among its bishops and divines. [Because your Church does not teach the truth. There is indeed no reason to glory in this discrepancy of teaching but rather to be ashamed of. It is as if a rambler boasted of his ragged dress. Forsooth, such discrepancy of teaching is a bad evidence of the Holy Ghost teaching your Church.] Yet what has been its career upon the whole? Which way has it been moving through three hundred years? [I will tell you. First it changed from Romanism to Calvinism; then from Calvinism to Laudism; then from Laudism to Sabellianism; then from Sabellianism to Paleyism; then followed the Evangelical Era; then the Anglo-Catholic Era; then . . . heaven knows what will follow . . . perhaps by and by a Colensonian Era. Bossuet's "Histoire des Variations des Eglises Protestantes" is generally known; not so the little book: "The Variations in the Church established by law, as traced in her past history and present condition; showing the diversities of faith compatible with the writings of her prelates and clergy." London, Ward & Co., 1846. I have nothing to do with the bias of the book, but its materials and quotations are suggestive of serious reflections.] Where does it find itself at the end? [At an unfathomable precipice.] Lutherans have tended to Rationalism; [and so have Anglicans; for what is the difference between Rationalism and Broad Churchism?] Calvinists have become Socinians; [and so have Anglicans. "Many of the clergy, amongst whom was .... Theophilus Lindsey, were satisfied to remain in the Church, and to use the Liturgy, under this modal hypothesis of the Trinity, *after they had become Unitarians* .... There is no doubt but that from the time of Dr. Clarke, Arianism, or more pure Unitarianism, became *the covert faith of the great body of the established clergy*, as appears by their printed sermons still extant, in which the marked absence of the doctrines of imputed righteousness, vicarious satisfaction, and other dogmas, before and since considered as the fundamental principles of orthodoxy, is quite obvious." The Variations in the Church, &c., p. 19, 20] but what has it become? [Answer: A queer medley of quarrelling parties; an instructive pattern-card of heresiology; a compendium of Protestant Church-history] Now, after above three centuries, it alone has a *more vigorous life than ever*. [An incredible infatuation—a *fata morgana* not uncommon in sandy deserts.]—We conclude the declamatory apostrophe of Dr. Pusey and his friend, and are, involuntarily, reminded of the saying: " Speech is given to hide the truth ; " not as if Dr. Pusey spoke against his conviction— we know

> He loves his Church's rule and order,
> And weeps to see her in disorder,
> Still true to first love, will not dare
> To leave her in her hour of care ;
> He feels that there is cause enow
> To pledge himself to former vow,
> To take his stand (though men rebel)*—

we know from his own mouth why he is still an Anglican: " What we learn earliest sinks the deepest :

> Quo semel est imbuta recens, servabit odorem
> Testa diu.

This we drank in when our minds were freshest," (The Real Presence. Oxford, 1857, p. 184); but it is quite inconceivable how Dr. Pusey and his friends feed upon Catholic antiquity, smuggling its doctrines into the Anglican Church, overlooking the emphatically Protestant character and history of the latter. Mr. Merle d'Aubigné delivered a lecture on the matter, which Rev. Bickersteth translated and prefaced, under the title " Geneva and Oxford." You will find there quotations from Pusey, Palmer, the late Froude and others, to the effect that they must *un-protestatize* the English Church, thus confessing themselves that the Church of the present day is Protestant, consequently fallen away from the truth, and to be left by those who wish to be Catholics. However let us be fair. It

* " What is a Puseyite ? " by a little Sprite. London, 1860, p. 26.

is a painful thing for an earnest Christian to see the untenableness of his Church, in which he has been born and bred. In sinking with his Church he catches hold of every straw. And such a straw is the pretended life in the English Church.

Aquesta vida es sueño!

Yes, this sacramental Church-life is a dream, a dream pregnant with mischief, in as far as it tends mystically to settle those minds which, by God's grace, felt unsettled. By showing the sacramental Church-life, Dr. Pusey withdraws from the bright daylight into the dark recess of mysticism, accessible only to spirits, either angels or devils. Here all rests on the feelings of the subject. This is the way how Mormons, Irvingites, and all the other mystical sects *prove irrefragably* the truth of their more or less blasphemous tenets. Dr. Pusey, it is true, produces facts, and chiefly one fact; I allude to the unworthy communicant who committed suicide (Eiren. p. 275). If his personal belief was in the Real Presence (though he did receive nothing but common bread and common wine), his act was sacrilegious, and the pangs of conscience might have driven him to suicide; but to take the fact as God's "awful judgment" is a still more awful word—a word which is condemned by Jesus Christ. " Judge not, that ye be not judged." (St. Matt. vii. 1.) It is a scandalous abuse of piety to judge others. I know only one man who is condemned in hell, viz. Judas, the son of perdition. Of all the rest of mankind God strictly forbids to judge. If this principle were observed more strictly by the so-called pious and godly Christians, there would be less scoffing and sneering at religion, to be sure. When Dr. Pusey infers from the above-mentioned suicide that the bread and wine received were the validly consecrated Eucharist, it is as much illogical as when he says (Eiren. p. 275) : " Presbyterians have what *they* believe [i. e. their Calvinistic heavenly Christ in the Lord's Supper]; we, what *we* believe" [we=the small body of Anglo-Catholics, opposite the overwhelming majority of Churchmen who are satisfied with naked Zwinglianism in the Lord's Supper.] How does Dr. Pusey know that? It is outright ridiculous to say: " Presbyterians *have* what *they* believe"—as if truth depended on human fancies. Would not, on this ground, Irvingites *have* what they believe, i. e. Apostles and Prophets?! On the whole, Dr. Pusey is fond of making assertions and putting them down as axioms, without even attempting to prove them. Now, most unfortunately, we are such matter-of-fact men as to ask for evidences, and to reject whatever is not substantiated. Everybody knows (and most likely Dr. Pusey also) how small a portion of the English Church believes in the Real Presence, in the efficacy of priestly Absolution, in the sacramental grace of Confirmation and Orders — and still he speaks of an organic and sacramental operation of the Holy Ghost upon the Church *as a whole !* However, logic is not commensurate to mysticism.

There is no organic life, *no Unity* in the English Church; and the Orthodox Church could not therefore find *the* Church to transact with; and even if she wished to transact, she could not find an Authority to ratify the compact. A national synod of the bishops under their head, the Primate of Canterbury, would be a fitting authority, it is true, but, alas! this Anglo-Catholic idea is both an *Anachronism* and an unlawful *Neology*. Let us pass by — there is no spiritual authority in the English Church.

But if all the Anglican bishops proved to be Intercommunionists, what then?

First, there is no fear of that. However, the case granted, the matter is very simple: the dissenting Churchmen would keep the Church and allow the bishops to retire. The bishops cannot, authoritatively, force upon their diocesans (clergy and laity) their private opinion and personal feeling. Nay, Parliament overrules them, and would set at nought their lofty schemes.

May the Orthodox Church enter into transactions with the English Church at large?

As long as you harbour *Heresy* in the bosom of your Church, without being able to *secrete* it from the system, either this system is *no Church at all* or a Church *infected, degenerated, and disabled by heresy*, an empty, hollow Church which the Holy Ghost has left. It is hard to choose one side of this sad alternative, but I know no sincere, pious, and open Orthodox Catholic can disavow that alternative. There is no mistake about that question. Let it only be put in such a concise, plain, and straightforward manner. The Orthodox Catholic Church does not recognize the English Church to be *a Church* in her own meaning of the word, no more than the Lutheran, Reformed, or any other Protestant Church. If we nevertheless use the term "Church" in the controversy, it is only a conventional mode of speaking, adopting the usual nomenclature of a "fait accompli," while disapproving the fact and denying the truth of the underlaid idea.

That there is heresy, plenty of heresy in the English Church, not heresy creeping in the dark, but open, boastful, clamorous heresy, *which the Church tolerates, since there are no means to get rid of the same* — this is a palpable fact which needs no demonstration.—The Broad Churchmen have no Bible, but only Hebrew, Chaldaic, Greek classics, Jewish standard works of very questionable authority. They abhor the Athanasian creed, and hate all dogmatic teaching. If they had to manage the business, the first thing would be to expunge the Athanasian creed, which is but a precise abstract of the five first œcumenical councils, compiled about the end of the sixth century. — The Evangelical watchword is "all-sufficiency of the Bible," and "general Priesthood," that is to say, exactly the same foundation as that of the Protestant dissenters. They somewhat value their Church as being a human bond, an imposing fabric, a magnificent establishment, whereas the dissenters are to be pitied for their loose and scattered position. The English "Church" is an aristocratic and national pride which pervades equally the minds of the wealthy and of the poor Churchmen, which pervades indiscriminately the minds of High, Low, and Broad Churchmen, however great the distance of their religious tenets may be. This *national feeling* is a *real bond*, but how little it has to do with religion, everybody knows. It ranks among the other noble passions of human frailty. But to return to the Evangelicals, they form a strong stock of the English Church. They have leading men of power and ability; and (which is highly creditable to them) they know what they are about; they have their fixed mark in view. So the late Canon Stowell was a staunch upholder of Evangelicalism in the Church. He said (" Abstract of report and speeches at the 29th annual meeting of the Church Pastoral-aid Society," May 5, 1864) : " I am convinced that we need not only to be vigilant and watchful against Latitudinarian tendencies, but against Romanizing tendencies. Be assured of it, we may have our attention so magnetized and concentrated by the one as to lose sight of the other. But I believe they are both tending to give advantage to that personage whom my friend (Canon Boyd) has traced as emerging out of the power of *sacerdotalism* into his vast and usurping ascendency. I believe the Jesuits are looking on behind the scenes, and rejoicing at Latitudinarianism not less than at Tractarianism" (pp. 13, 14): "Let us not be chilled in our love to her (viz. the Church). We love her all the more, because we believe that, *as she has braved the storm of Sacerdotalism and* SACRAMENTALISM (!!), *so she will brave the storm of subtle Latitudinarianism*" (p. 15). Now I ask

Dr. Pusey: Did you disclaim Church-communion with Canon Stowell who denounced *Sacerdotalism* and *Sacramentalism*? Or do you not consider this denunciation heretical? Differing religious *opinions* were and ever will be in the Church; but here is more than opinions; here are *dogmas* at stake, *vital* principles on which depends the very existence of the Church. But—mark the inconsistency!—even advanced Anglo-Catholics are not so particular in this respect. They regard Evangelicalism as a legitimate shade of Church-teaching, betraying their indifference concerning Catholic truth. Catholicity must be *exclusive* of any admixture of heresy. Now the Anglo-Catholics do not approve of Evangelical teaching, and still they continue Church-communion with the Evangelicals. No true Catholic would do such a thing. However the Anglo-Catholics (at least Dr. Pusey and his friends) are half-Evangelicals, since they believe in the "all-sufficiency of the Bible." Eiren. p. 95, we read of "a tendency (among Catholics) to hold cheaply by Holy Scripture, as being comparatively unimportant to them, who have the authority of an infallible Church, forgetting *that the authority of the Church depends upon Holy Scripture.*" To this the reply is to be found in "the Month" (December, 1865), p. 625: "It would be difficult to explain . . . the object of the long note filled with quotations from the Fathers about the faith being contained in the Scriptures, unless it be to give an impression that Dr. Pusey's adversaries—Catholics of course—differ from the Fathers on this point. It is quite as easy to prove from the Fathers—almost as easy from many of Dr. Pusey's own quotations—that they most fully recognized tradition, and the authority of the Church as the guardian of Scripture. Dr. Pusey knows, as well as he knows anything, that the Fathers *do not in the least support the notion that the "faith is contained in the Scriptures" in any sense in which Catholics deny it and Protestants maintain it.*" Thus Anglo-Catholicism is a semi-Evangelical sect confessing the "all-sufficiency of the Bible;" but at the same time it is strongly anti-Evangelical, since it maintains the sacerdotal character of the English Church, which sacerdotalism (implying sacramentalism) is a horror to the Evangelicals, an apostasy from Gospel truth, an abominable heresy. The author of "the Variations in the Church," &c., is, therefore, quite right in saying (p. 40): "While the Evangelical party felt confident that in the records of the English Church they had found ample proof of their principles being the true standard of English orthodoxy, their opponents with equal confidence gleaned, from the same records, the most satisfactory confirmation of their views being the only true and orthodox belief. Alas! said our Enquirer,

'Who with another's eye can read?
Or worship by another's creed?'

And yet each of these opposite parties, taking their own eyes alone as the unerring standard of other men's perceptions, unhesitatingly condemn .... all who cannot see, think, and believe, just as they do." And again (p. 5): "Our Enquirer could not help remarking the obviously direct incompatibility between the new Protestant Articles, and the High Church and priestly claims of the Creeds and other formularies derived from the Romish Church, and still retained in the Liturgy, Rubrics, &c., of the newly reformed Church; and he wondered how such ill-assorted elements could have been expected ever to work well together. That they had not done so was proved by following the stream of time, which exhibited these discordant principles at perpetual variance, and showed the alternate ascendency, at one time of the Articles over the Liturgy, and at another of the Liturgy over the Articles; and thus forming a sort of high and low Church barometer, indicative of the changeable atmosphere in which the newly reformed Church was destined to live and move and have her being." No other Protestant Church was ever so full of contradictions, so full of variegated heresy, as the English Church was, and is, and will be to the end of her existence. With *such an heretical Church* the Orthodox Church never would allow her bishops to transact. With *individuals* belonging to the English Church she will be most happy to treat, but an *English Church* she does not know, and may not know, as long as she preserves pure Orthodoxy. It is significant that the Romish Church pretends to be *the* CATHOLIC *Church*, priding herself in *numbers;* on the contrary, the Eastern Church calls herself emphatically *the* ORTHODOX *Church*, knowing that Catholicity without Orthodoxy is good for nothing, but Orthodoxy necessarily implies Catholicity. The

Orthodox Church always watched *the pure immaculate belief*, watched it with the utmost concern of a fond lover; despised poverty, sword, torture inflicted by an infidel master; lost everything except the pure faith, "counting all things but loss for the excellency of the knowledge of Christ Jesus" which is only to be found in pure belief; laughed at the sneers of the wise of this world; resisted both the flatteries and the persecutions of heretical emperors; stood firm when the Pope of Rome apostatized from the truth, involving half the Christendom in his ignominious fall, delivering up his fellow Christians to the iron rod of Muhammed's disciples, when he could have saved them, sacrificing the cross to the crescent, out of mere spitefulness, because the Easterns declined to desert the standard of Catholic truth, and would not accept the novel pretensions of divine right based on insatiable human pride and presumption. There she stands—the Holy Orthodox Church—like the adamantine rock of ages. Romanists and Protestants decry her as *petrified*, because she refuses to move from the place where Christ has fixed her; because she will not descend to human innovations; because she will not divest herself of her divine privileges. For these reasons both her enemies hate *and envy* her, for she is a *living reproof* to both of them; she is the voice of History written in a lapidary style outliving a thousand years, and no letter is altered or vanished, since the finger of God had written them and no man! What has the Orthodox Church to glory in? Has she a pompous history of Popes who ruled the world? Has she a Legion of diversified religious orders? Has she an almighty order of Jesuits who like crossspiders spin their cobwebs all over the world, in the church-doors, in the confessionals, as well as in the ante-chambers and boudoirs? Has she a lot of monarchs to protect and support her? Has she a Canon-Law like Rome? A canon-law, an exquisite tissue of subtilty, craftiness, and loquacity? No, she has nothing but *a pure faith*, and besides poverty and singleness of heart! Oh, there arose temptations to the Orthodox Church, greater than man could stand. Rome took her up into an exceeding high mountain, and showed her all the kingdoms of the world, and the glory of them; and said unto her: All these things will I give thee, if thou wilt fall down and worship me. But she said: Get thee hence! I will go on penniless and friendless—my only friend and comfort is Christ's pure faith, my only staff and shield is Christ's pure faith. Then came Sloth and Indifference, the fatal companions of want and poverty. Love and Charity gave way, and ruder passions trespassed on God's holy commandments—but nobody dared to touch the pure faith. Then came the fiend, a cynical scoff on his lips, sowing Voltaire's and Rousseau's tares; and infidelity and superstition, levity and credulity, wickedness and despair, sprung up like the prophet's gourd—but nobody touched the faith. Infidelity did not enter the Church, but left it alone. Comes the Eastern Church Association, offers her substantial assistance. Comes

Dr. Pusey and says (Eiren. p. 263): "Our position gives us an advantage towards her (the Greek Church) also; because, while we are widespread enough to be no object of contempt (!?), there can be no dread on either side of any interference with the self-government of each." The Orthodox Church says: "We do not want your power nor your riches—these are no baits for us—we are content with our poverty and with our pure faith which nobody shall sully. And are we to commune with a Church *so replete of heresy* as the English Church is! Are we to expose *our only treasure, our pure faith*, to such a calamity! True, heresy may arise and *be concealed*, for a time, in the Orthodox Church, but as soon as it shows itself openly, *it is directly and without delay cast out* in order to preserve the body whole. But you—you have installed heresy on your pulpits; you do not cast it out; nay, you *cannot* cast it out, because your Church is historically a Protestant Church, and Protestants framed your Articles which you contrive in vain to unprotestantize. *God forbid! No communion with an heretical Church! No communion with the English Church—it would be the grave of Orthodoxy!!!* What communion hath light with darkness?* Woe unto them that put darkness for light, and light for darkness;† that say: Peace, peace, when there is no peace.‡ Behold, for peace they have great bitterness.§ Think not that our Lord came to send peace on earth; he came not to

---

* 2 Cor. vi. 14.   † Isa. v. 20.
‡ Jerem. vi. 14.   § Isa. xxxviii. 17.

send peace, but a sword.* He came to send fire on the earth;† and if your fabric is not fire-proof; if you have built upon the foundation, which is Jesus Christ, hay and stubble, your work shall be burned.‡ As yet your feet stumble upon the dark mountains, and, while ye look for light, blind not yourselves, lest He turn it into the shadow of death, and make it gross darkness.§ The light shineth forth from Orthodoxy; but the light shineth in darkness, and the darkness comprehended it not.‖ Still you wait for light, but behold obscurity; for brightness, but you walk in darkness. You grope for the wall like the blind, and you grope as if you had no eyes; you stumble at noonday as in the night; you are in desolate places as dead men. You roar all like bears, and mourn sore like doves: you look for judgment, but there is none; for salvation, but it is far off from you.¶ Thus saith the Lord: Stand ye in the ways, and see, *and ask for the old paths, where is the good way, and walk therein, and ye shall find rest for your souls.*" **

Every one who believes in a visible Church, however poor his idea of the Church may be, feels *the necessity of Unity and Intercommunion* between its several branches. So much the more so at a time when unbelief raises its head and threatens to desolate the Church. You look for assistance; you strengthen your position; you fortify your weak points; and you discover from how many points your

* St. Matt. x. 34. † St. Luke xii. 49.
‡ 1 Cor. iii. 11—15. § Jer. xiii. 16. ‖ St. John i. 5.
¶ Isa. lix. 9—11. ** Jer. vi. 16.

fortress is assailable. You have plenty of work to do *within*, in order to repair and restore the Church to its ancient glory and power. You have plenty of work to do *without*, in order to find the way, by which you might enter into the visible communion with the Catholic churches. You send your learned men to the different quarters of the Catholic Church, that they may bring about a mutual understanding. You write and read about your own Church and about those with which you like to commune. You discuss, publicly and privately, the matter at issue.

All these efforts are creditable to the promoters of a work which proceeds from a good intention. However, a good work may be misunderstood and mismanaged. I may be allowed, therefore, to add a few general remarks and strictures on the subject.

"There is a conventional homage due to all attempts at reconciliation and union, however abortive or utterly hopeless, and we should be sorry to break the good old custom. We can only regret that this purely conventional homage is all that we can render to" the said efforts. Those discussions are merely a friendly exchange of opinions, showing that in some quarters of the English Church an Intercommunion with any recognized Catholic Church is wished for. The invitation comes from the English Church, not from the Orthodox Church. This is a remarkable fact suggestive of the question: Why is it that the Orthodox Church, whose longing for reunion of Christendom is world-known, is waiting quietly till matters change, while the English Church shows, in attaining this end, an uneasiness indicative of certain misgivings as to her foundation and constitution, being insulated and not recognized by any Catholic Church? Hence the hasty course which even Bishops recommended. They "urged that, in their opinion, we should not content ourselves with preparing the ground, leaving the harvest to be reaped by future generations, but *deferring all dogmatical debates*, proceed to celebrate the Lord's Supper by intercommunion, if such were the wish of the chiefs of our Church." That is not a parliamentary course of proceeding; that is neither a judicial nor judicious way to bring a union about. First, I think, we must know whether the two parties are *unitable*; then we ask *how* they are to be united; lastly, we *conclude* the Union; and the first act of this concluded Union is the holy *Communion*. I think plain common sense marks out these successive stages of proceeding. As yet the question stands in the first stage, discussing the *Unitability* or the Harmony of Faith and fundamental Church-constitution; or rather the question *ought* to stand in this first stage, and not to leap precipices, anticipating the end before having passed the first stage. The Anglicans, most significantly, apprehend the sifting cross-examination in the first stage, as you will see from the Canada correspondence of "the Churchman" (Jan. 4, 1866): "The desire after unity, especially with the Greek Church, appears to be steadily progressing in the United States, and one of the

CATHOLIC ORTHODOXY. 101

Clergy of the Diocese of Huron lately proposed a resolution expressive of the same hopes, but did not bring it forward in Synod, as upon inquiry he found *that a large portion of the Diocese was not yet prepared to receive it*... It appears to me that the only proper course (? !) to adopt is to receive each other's members to the sacred rites of our respective Churches on the simple ground of their membership and good standing in their own branch of the Church Catholic. Anything more is surely inconsistent with all correct Church principle. Greek or Anglican, the individual should certainly be received by the Sister Church, *not on the ground of correctness of his private opinions,** but from the fact of his being an accredited member of a valid branch of the Church Catholic." But if so, there is no more propriety in questioning him on his private judgment concerning certain, often obtuse, questions, than there would be in examining a parishioner from Islington upon his views of Baptismal Regeneration, or the Real Presence, before we admitted him to the privileges of the Church in our own parishes.† If we go beyond this general

---

* What the writer understands by "*private opinions*" we see afterwards when he speaks of Baptismal Regeneration and the Real Presence. Anglo-Catholicism is so deeply Protestant, that it never will learn to distinguish between *inalienable dogmas* and *private school opinions*.

† Just the contrary is the case in the Orthodox Church. If a communicant does not believe Baptismal Regeneration, or the Real Presence, the priest *must* refuse him the Lord's Supper; and if he doubts of the communicant's belief, he *must* question him, or he will both be an accomplice of heterodoxy and incur the censure of the Church.

acknowledgment of each other's communion as being essentially valid portions of the "One Catholic and Apostolic Church," *rely upon it, we shall get into inextricable difficulties.* More than this, will on both sides infringe on individual liberty, or cause parties to *condone what they cannot but consider serious, though not damnable error,** and nothing less than the latter should prevent intercommunion." "*Deferring all dogmatical debates.*" This is an instructive sentence which suffices to lay bare the character of Anglo-Catholicism holding cheaply by the first requisite of Catholicity, viz. "true faith" (ὀρθὴ δόξα). Do you think the *Orthodox* Church is to accept her partner without looking into the matter and previously ascertaining whether this partner is not *heterodox*? Mixed marriages and misalliances never proved happy, and divorce is a sad thing. However, the Orthodox Church is cautious, and never tampered with youthful passions; and the English Church (or rather the few Intercommunionist members of her) must feel thankful to the Orthodox Church for not over-hurrying the matter. For,

Likewise St. Athanasius would have refused the holy communion to an Homoiusian. But would Dr. Pusey have refused the Lord's Supper to Canon Stowell, who denounced sacerdotalism and sacramentalism, and published a volume of sermons against the vital doctrines of Catholicism, under the title: "Tractarianism tested"? This shows the genuine indifference of Protestant Anglo-Catholicism.

* My Orthodox friends, take notice of this. You hold " *serious errors*," and if the English Church would "*condone*" them, she would "*get into inextricable difficulties.*" Now you know what you have to think and hope of the English compliments of union. They only wish to extend their acquaintance, but, respecting the Orthodox Faith and holy Canons, they will have nothing to do with you.

after the conclusion of peace, the war would begin and place the Intercommunionists in an awkward dilemma. Fancy the bulk of the English Church, which is just now crying aloud against the tame and feeble attempts of High-Churchism to introduce a few Ritualistic innovations—this very bulk of Churchmen should enter a Greek Church, being told their Church and the Greek were essentially the same. They see pictures, standards, priestly garments, crosses, candles, incense, holy water, crossing, kissing of relics, &c.—shocking indeed for the jejune taste of those soi-disant pure Gospel-Christians! They would sneer at those who would make them believe that the two churches were one. A regular war and disruption of the English Church would ensue—and then only you would see how *intensely Protestant* the majority of the English Church is. To predict this result we need, indeed, no prophetical gift. The Anglo-Catholics boast of their gaining ground—of course, they hear no other opinions but their own, as the Low and Broad-Churchmen do not apply to them, whom they consider masked papists. This is the matter-of-fact view, rather discouraging for High Churchmen, but, after all, alarmingly true and correct.—In some desperate cases it may be expedient to break down or burn the bridge behind one. Well, where is that great Captain who, with the weight of his colossal genius, will overpower the unity of Churchmen, muffle the mouth of Private Judgment, strike a blow bewildering Protestant mankind, and thunder out his determination: I will you to be Catholics! We have no Savanarola; but were he born, he would be of no avail against Protestantism. Luther was a mighty man; he thundered down Papacy, but when the waves of Private Judgment threatened to sweep Christianity away, his power was gone. Such a Captain is a dream, and his army is *Hope forlorn.* "The Times" says: "The Church of England is the United Church of England and Ireland, and, harsh as the expression may seem, it is nevertheless . . . *a creature of the law.*" Mr. Palmer tried, and all the Anglo-Catholics try, to divest the Church of this ominous characteristic, or at least to declare it harmless, not affecting the substance of the Church. How they can maintain this assertion in spite of the explicit expressions of the law, which claims *spiritual* power, nobody can understand besides the Anglo-Catholics, and most likely they do not understand it themselves. To the English Church the State is something more than the impressed stamp to "The Times." Let us suppose the Anglo-Catholics had brought about a union with the Orthodox Church, would it be a union of the Orthodox *and English* Church without sanction of the government, without Act of Parliament? "The Times" proceeds: "The Russian Church is also a State Church, *like our own.*" And "The Churchman" assents. In this both are eminently wrong. There is a lawful, necessary, and expedient bond between Church and State (for we are not Cavourian Utopists); but the State is not to overrule the Church in spirituals. The State has a "jus *circa* sacra;" it may look into the secular administration, into the money matters, &c., of the Church, as of any other public institution within the State. The State, however, has no "jus *in* sacra," may not interfere in spirituals, as it is the case in the English Church. A "Gorham case," the erection of a Lutheran-Anglican bishopric by the crown, the proceedings against the Essays and Reviews, and against Bishop Colenso, are occurrences *inconceivable* and *impossible* in the Orthodox Church. From this follows, 1. That the Emperor of Russia *is not and never was the head of the Russian Church*, he holds no *Supremacy* in the Church; 2. The Emperor is, with regard to settling and interpreting the Faith and holy Canons, as impotent as any other layman. He cannot alter a jot in the deposit of Faith; 3. The Emperor would, in spite of his autocratic power, be unable (e. g.) to obtrude on the Church a single clergyman of Broad Church principles. The Bishops would refuse him, and— the Emperor have to yield; 4. " Articles of Religion" imposed *by Act of Parliament* would have been declined by all the Russian clergy. They would have considered such an act both ridiculous and usurping; 5. The Russian loves his Orthodox Emperor as a child loves his father, and the Russian Church likewise bows to the Emperor in filial love and devotion. But let the Emperor cease to be Orthodox; let him allow an Heterodox influence to take place—what will happen? Revolve the pages of history; there you may read it. Not where Church and State are blended, as in the Papal State (indeed an exemplary State ! ?), but where both act in harmony, as in the Russian Empire, their beneficial influence and sincere mutual devotion are manifest. Thus the Russian State is rather subject to Orthodoxy than Orthodoxy to the State. The Russian Church is, therefore, neither a "State engine," nor the State a Church engine, but both Church and State are pervaded by the same spirit, linked by a solidarity of interests.

The Churchmen who set the Intercommunion movement on foot, irrespective of any settled doctrinal basis, gained nothing by it, absolutely nothing, not even the consciousness of the eternal gulf between both Churches, which, by the by, would have been a real gain, as it would prevent people from making preposterous attempts to unite two disparate parties, not unitable as long as both rest on their present foundations. We do not know what "The Churchman" means by these words: "Some few 'Extremists' in the Eastern Church, who are tainted with the Jesuit teaching (!), which was so profusely poured into Constantinople two centuries ago, may feel in this way (i. e. unfavourably to Intercommunion); but the majority are liberal, open to reasoning, and fair beyond expectation to the claims of Anglo-Catholics, though they feel *still* [and *ever* will feel!] bound by the spirit of their ancient traditions." Jesuitism, being the opposite pole of Orthodoxy, never entered the Eastern Church. But I fear "The Churchman" calls the staunch champions of Orthodoxy, who explode Protestantism in any shape (also under a Catholicising disguise), Jesuits. Liberalism, with its elastic notions of truth, is unknown to the Orthodox clergy. The words: In Russia "the Anglican Church is highly popular, as far as it is known and understood," are simply to be changed into: "as far as it is *not* known and *not* understood." The only reason why the Orthodox are more friendly to the Anglicans than to any other Protestants is their good will and their upright longing for Catholic truth. This cements a friendship between *individuals*, not between their Churches. The English Church is Protestant, and therefore *null;* there does not exist an English *Church* in the eyes of the Orthodox Church. No transaction, no compromise, no bartering about dogmas. In this respect "the Eastern is an absolutely *iron system.*" Full and explicit Orthodoxy is required as the first requisite of partnership. "We ask with all submission, *Why this move in the direction of the Russian Church?* Of course it is not uncommon for people to think that their own neighbours are the very worst in the whole world, and that they could find very much better neighbours by going a little farther off, and beating up some new quarter." This remark of "The Times" shows a great ignorance of the whole affair. The Orthodox movement within the English Church originated from men entirely conversant with Orthodoxy as early as 1716. They did not try the Orthodox, because they found the Roman-Catholics inflexible, but because they saw that Rome had lost the pure Catholic faith. The present movement, it is true, has not such clear views; otherwise a considerable number of Anglican clergymen would not have compromised themselves and presented to the world the most ludicrous spectacle in applying to the Pope for general Intercommunion between the East and the West, between Papists, Anglicans, and Orthodox. They had to pocket a sharp rebuff from Rome; and the East was astonished at the *naïveté* and gross ignorance of such men. Who, on the part of the East, had commissioned them? Is it not dogmatical indifference undervaluing doctrinal differences? "We do not want controversy, we want Intercommunion," says the Churchman; which would be about the same as if a man wished to be your partner in business but declined all other particulars. Let us first examine your books, whether you are not perhaps a bankrupt. Still the present Orthodox movement is not an expletive of failure in Romish transactions. The Orthodox Church is *really more liberal* than Rome (which is only satisfied by *entire submission*), whereas it requires Unity of faith and of fundamental Church constitution, but does not enforce *Uniformity* (as Rome does). An Anglican Church in Western garb would be recognized by the Orthodox Church, provided all the Doctrines and Holy Canons, the Apostolical foundation and succession were established. The actual English Church does not possess these requisites; a *future Anglican Church*, to be recruited not only from amongst the members of the actual Church, but from Papists and Protestants generally, to be built up on Orthodox basis, but preserving its Western peculiarity and national independence, will be recognized by the East. We ask once more: "Why this move?" Why this cry for Intercommunion? We answer: It is nothing but the uneasy feeling of Isolation. The English Church is not, and never was, recognized by any Catholic Church. This *indisputable fact* weighs so heavy in the scales of all unprejudiced minds as to unsettle them and to expose them to serious doubts. Is not Dr. Pusey's Eirenicon a spasmodic struggle against this feeling? Is not every assurance, that he feels perfectly easy and at rest, a suppressed cry: I wish I were at rest? My Anglican brethren, stop here awhile, and ponder these words.

It is remarkable that the Anglo-Catholics are so incredibly short-sighted as to *identify the English Church with their own limited party in the Church.* Even if they were at the helm (which they are not) it would be quite insignificant. But let us consider the Anglo-Catholic subdivision of the English Church *separately and as a whole* (although it would be by no means easy to draw a line of demarcation between the parties; and even in the camp of the Anglo-Catholics there are strong shades of opinions and doctrines which would soon prove irreconcilable). How far and how long would (e. g.) the two champions Dr. Pusey and Dr. Neale agree? The Anglo-Catholics form a *Coalition*, which it would be difficult to *sublime* into a *Church;*

   And he who understands it would be able
   To add a story to the Tower of Babel.

"We will suppose" (says "The Weekly Register") "that not only Dr. Pusey, but a large body who are willing to be represented by him, are prepared for *bonâ fide* negotiations for reunion, . . . but here occurs a difficulty, so great as to be almost overwhelming. Dr. Pusey represents, as yet, *only a School of opinion*. Not one English Bishop has publicly identified himself with this School, and few of the Anglican Bishops ever lose an opportunity of publishing their energetic dissent from many of the doctrines, which Dr. Pusey and those who think with him, hold as integral portions of the Faith." The *Christian Remembrancer* says : " Within the English Church there exists a large School, who look upon the desire to unite with Rome [and with the Orthodox Church] in any form as *sinful*, and who must *pari passu* be conciliated, unless the unity of Christendom is to determine the break-up of the Church of England." The writer of the Sermon: "Difficulties of Reunion" (Sermon IX. in the New Series of Sermons on the Reunion of Christendom. Hayes : London, 1865) comments thus on the words quoted : "We have no desire to make light of this very serious consideration, and no honest discussion of our present subject can escape its force and urgency. There are, it may be, some among us who would make short work with it. They would regard the expulsion of the so-termed Evangelicals from the Church as a blessing only inferior to the reunion of Catholic-minded Churchmen with the Latin and Greek communions. We cannot agree with them in this judgment." Dr. Pusey is of the same opinion, but "the union, such as it is, between Dr. Pusey and the Evangelicals, can only be made real and lasting by *a growing indifference to sound doctrine*" ("The Month" Dec. 1865, p. 637). We subjoin two more passages from "The Month" (Dec. 1865), p. 622: "We need only repeat, that he (sc. Dr. Pusey) defends Anglicanism on grounds which would probably be repudiated by every single bishop on the bench, by nine hundred and ninety out of every thousand of her clergy, and by the laity in the same proportion." And again, p. 623: "What would be the use of considering proposals which would be at once disavowed by those in whose name they are made? Unless Dr. Pusey thinks and speaks as the head of a party in the Establishment, *which would act for itself*, it is difficult to see how he can suppose it to be of any use to make such statements." We conclude with a passage from "The Weekly Register": "The national Church, *as a body*, can make no advances which could be accepted by the (Roman-)Catholic authorities, or even by the Oriental or Russian Communions, *because it can have no authoritative voice*, or common principle, or moral personality, there would be *no one to treat or to be treated with*. It must continue a heterogeneous body so long as it does not put from it one of the two great Schools which have always held divided sway. How then, meantime, will that School in the Anglican Church, supposing it to be able legally to hold its ground, be able to do so conscientiously, should its members have advanced so far individually, as to be ready to seek for corporate reunion, on the principles of Bossuet and the Gallican divines?" We endorse the opinion of the Roman-Catholic paper, and see no other expedient for the Anglo-Catholics than, before all, *to leave the actual Church.* Then only could we find a *Corporation to treat with.*

Thus Intercommunion is neither wanted by, nor possible to, the English Church as a whole. It is equally impossible to the party that set the present movement on foot, as long as it remains a part of the whole.

No Intercommunion but Reunion!

REUNION

presupposes a schism; and a schism is generally the fruit of a deeper misunderstanding than mere disciplinary quarrels. Schism and heresy set in, as soon as a person or a body tampers with novel doctrines, relaxes the bond of the Church, or lays hands upon its sacred privileges. Where, at first, only schism was intended and the work began with pure schism, in the long run heresy crept in, in order to make full, as it were, the vial of God's wrath.

The English Church separated from Rome. We have no reason to blame her for that, since Rome itself was schismatically separated from the East. If England's schism had proved a *Repristination of true Catholic principles,* it would have been a blessing to herself and to all Western Catholic Christendom. The East would have hastened to embrace her sister-church, and to support the great work of occidental Reunion. Alas! the Anglican Church, after having shaken off Rome's fetters, fell in with the Reformers, and was carried off, far away from Catholic ground, by the fluctuations of Private Judgment. It is true, there is a strong Catholic feature in the English character, which even three centuries of Protestant influence could not efface, and which made of Anglicanism a strange compound of Protestantism and Catholicism. This feature is *the innate Traditional and Conservative disposition of the English mind* sticking to History as the living foundation of nations and of all their vital institutions. The German mind is inclined to soar in ideal spheres far above the real life here below. Philosophical conceptions, subjective fancies are to replace the matter-of-fact reality. Luther was the chief incarnation and representative of this German mind, and the Father of Protestantism. Had Luther kept the historical ground of the Catholic Church; had he dived into the vast depths of Dogmas divinely taught and heartily to be embraced—he might have become a Father of the Church, a Father mightier than many a faithful philosopher and profound divine in by-gone ages, a popular Father of the Catholic people at large. But Luther, emancipating the *Subject* from the *objective* ground and condition of mankind rooted in History, became the curse and scourge of his race. The English had enough German blood in their veins to follow with curiosity the progress of Reformation, but not enough to break thoroughly with the past, to strip themselves of everything substantial. The English people never introduced Reformation; it was imposed upon them and, so to say, "*octroyée*" by unprincipled tyrants supported by a handful of innovators. But in spite of tyranny and persecution the English would not part with their Church; and only when something like a Church, some delusive phantom, was presented to their eyes, they were duped into what they considered their ancient Church cleansed from Popish rubbish. This is the real history of the English Reformation; and the inconsistency of Anglicanism is but its glory and hope in the eyes of all true Catholics. It is gratifying to muse on the English Church, and to think that this is the only Protestant body which tenaciously clung to the idea of the Catholic *Church*. All Protestant sects, indeed, claim for themselves Catholicity; but none, except the Anglicans, think, at least to a certain extent, to be saved by the instrumentality of their Church. Hence the more intense Catholic feeling of the Anglicans; hence their yearning towards Reunion with the rest of Catholic Christendom.

But *where is the Catholic Church?* This is naturally the first question of all serious Anglican Reunionists. Is it the Eastern or the Western Church? Both do not agree; both disclaim one another's title to sound Catholicity. Both cannot go together. Therefore the wise Reunionist knows he must choose.

CATHOLIC ORTHODOXY.

In some quarters of the Anglican Church there exists a signal propensity to *Rome*. This is easily to be accounted for. 1. Roman Catholics surround and influence the Anglicans. They are scattered about all over the country. Their churches, sermons, lectures are attended by Anglicans. A Roman Hierarchy has drawn a net-work over the country, and has both practically set at nought the Anglican Hierarchy, and practically decided the invalidity of Anglican Ordinations. Thus the Roman Catholics have settled down in England, and feel quite at home. Churches, Convents, Educational Establishments supply their wants. They have their Lords, their Members of Parliament—in short, they form an influential part of Society. 2. The Anglican Church springing from the Roman has preserved many points of contact available to re-unite the parties. 3. The Western Catholic mind is, as yet, only represented by the Roman Catholic Church. And the Eastern mind has a very different stamp. Although the same Catholic truth existed, for many centuries, undefiled in both portions of Christ's Church, still *the individual frame of mind, the characteristics of both the East and the West* were by God's will and providence always differing, as their respective countries and nations are different. 4. The Eastern Church is far off, and, just on account of her distance, is more like an ideal Church, intangible, inaccessible to our grasp. "Aus den Augen, aus dem Sinn " is a true German proverb. We like what is near and palpable; it stares at us till we are charmed into its embrace.

Such is the spell of every "*fait accompli*" before our eyes. You curse the Kingdom of Italy, but you cannot help recognizing it.—Now let us view Romanism, whether its claims to true and sound Catholicism hold good or not.

ROMANISM.

THE sad event of the schism dividing the East and the West has one striking feature confounding Rome's claims to pure Catholicity. It is the wonderful fidelity and adherence of the East to its Church. Rome's pretensions found the East resisting to a man. The whole clergy and laity withstood unflinching. The Eastern Church remained what it was, neither losing ground, nor altering its faith and holy canons. And when the vain attempt of the Council of Florence was made, it appeared to the world once more, how the whole Eastern Church is *fundamentally* opposed to Romanism.—It is not so with the schism which, at a later period, Reformation brought about within the pale of the Roman Church. Then only *individuals* separated; there was no *compact body* which continued holding its ancient belief and as such was cut off from Rome. The Romans like to compare both these schisms, in order to put a slur upon these Easterners. But truth is so irresistible that even Romanism must admit of the invariableness of the Eastern Church; while the Western Church moved on in her self-chosen track, one-sided, independent, self-sufficient, presuming to represent the Universal Church, developing her system into novel doctrines, thus combining arrogance with corruption.

Our defence of Orthodoxy can, according to the limited plan of this book, only be short. We cannot enter into details. We confine ourselves to an exposition of the *Spirit of Romanism*.

Latet alto in pectore vulnus.

This fatal wound is Papacy. By Papacy we understand the doctrine that the Pope is *divino jure* the Head of the Church and the Vicar of Christ. The Catholic Church granted the first place among the bishops to the bishop of Rome (who with that of Alexandria shared the title of "Pope"). Rome, the capital of the world, took precedence; and Constantinople, the second capital, obtained the second place. Thus it was the important position of the two bishops which determined their rank. The Roman Pope never was the divinely instituted head of the Church, but only its ecclesiastically instituted Primate. The Roman commentators explain the Rock on which the Church was built (St. Matt. xvi. 18) as signifying St. Peter and his successors on the see of Rome. And the German Bible of Allioli (*approved by the Pope*) adds in a note: "This is the consonant teaching of *all* the holy Fathers." It is scarcely conceivable how a divine, who compiled a commentary from the Fathers, could make such a flagrant misstatement; since the *overwhelming majority* of the Fathers understands the Rock of St. Peter's belief in the Divinity of Christ.

Is this not an irrefragable proof that this majority of Fathers did not know nor believe that St. Peter was the Rock on which the Church was built? And if the majority of the Fathers did not know it, they were not taught so. Dr. Newman might plead here the "Doctrinal Development" in the Church. But this doctrine of the Rock, on which the Church is built, belonged to the very essentials of the foundation of the Church. The foundation of the building *cannot be developed* any more, as soon as the structure is erected upon it. We should first have to undo what we have done in order to reach the foundation. Had the Apostles recognized in St. Peter the divinely instituted head of the Church, to be sure, all the Apostolical Churches would have transmitted such a fundamental truth of Church Constitution, and no Father would have ignored it. But did the Apostles neither know nor teach it (although the Church was built, and, consequently, nothing lacking in its foundation), this doctrine was *imported and not developed*. Romanists may discover in the New Testament and early Church History all sorts of hints of St. Peter's Supremacy; they may interpret expressions of devotion and affection as signs of submission; the direct teaching of the Fathers shows better than anything else that the Pope of Rome was not what, in later times, he pretended to be, and strove to become. Had St. Cyprian lived at our times, he would not only not be considered a Saint, but Rome would have excommunicated him and placed his books on the Index. The germ of the Pope's Supremacy is fast developing as early as the fall of the Western empire, or rather as early as its decline, when the Pope extended his power in a quasi-masterless country. *Crescit eundo.* The increase of practical power (both spiritual and secular), and the securing of its permanency, necessitated Popedom to look for a *doctrinal basis*, the utilisation of which could still extend the power existing. And so it was. History shows us how Episcopal rights were, bit by bit, swallowed up by Papal usurpation; how Lainez, general of the Jesuits, plainly maintained in the Council of Trent that all Episcopal power was vested in the Pope, and was to be derived from the Pope. Insatiable greediness palliated by a cloak of divine right is the awful characteristic of Papacy. He who is not deaf to the voice of history will discover this eminently human tissue of imperiousness and oppression. We do not allude to the Pope as secular prince; we only regard his ecclesiastical government. Do we not find the same or rather a greater arrogance in the Encyclicals and the Syllabus of the present Pope than in the documents of Innocent III.?

Let it be understood that the Orthodox Church recognizes, conformably to the canons of the Œcumenical Councils of Nice, Constantinople, and Chalcedon, the *Ecclesiastical Primacy* of the see of Rome, but rejects its *Divine Primacy* or *Supremacy* as an human innovation contrary to the true Catholic tradition. It is astounding to see the amount of confidence with which Roman divines advance their doctrine on the Pope, tracing it back to the Apostolic age, twisting Holy Scripture according to the Protestant rule of Private Judgment, instead of interpreting the same by the voice of lawful tradition as found in the holy Fathers; imposing upon the superficial student by quotations from the Fathers, which, torn from their context and disfigured by unwarrantable misinterpretations, are paraded to make up for the want of a solid traditional basis. A lot of pseudonymous works, written for the purpose of supporting the doctrine of Papacy, attributed to the most important Fathers* are now discarded, it is true; but must not the observation strike the reader that among the many apocryphical works of the middle ages by far the greater part treats about Rome's Supremacy and its privileges? If Rome's Supremacy is so clearly stated by the Fathers, as the Papists affect, why should one undertake the gratuitous labour not only to look for more supports but to *forge* them? Commonly such means are considered most desperate expedients to prevent the ruin of a tottering fabric.

How the Romans conceive the origin and progress of the Papal Supremacy, and how the Ortho-

---

* Compare *Thomas James* "On the Corruption of Scripture, Councils, and Fathers by the Prelates, Pastors, and Pillars of the Church of Rome, for the Maintenance of Popery." Revised and corrected from the editions of 1612 and 1688, by the Rev. J. E. Cox, M.A. London, 1843.

dox impugn it I have shown in another place.* Still we must confess that in the last years the naïve and unhistoric conception of Papacy as a ready-made institution of the primitive Church has, within the pale of the Romish Church, lost much of its ground. Dr. Newman develops it out of very faint outlines, and Mr. Allies ("Dr. Pusey and the Ancient Church," London, 1866, p. 68 *seq.*) applies to them the key of the saying of the fourth Council: ".. your Holiness, the very person *intrusted by the Saviour with the Guardianship of the Vine*" (p. 54). Mr. Allies proceeds: "But *how* was Pope Leo intrusted *by the Saviour* with this Guardianship? ... Had anything unusual taken place in his instance, with reference to which it could be said that Christ Himself had intrusted him with the Vine? Nothing; he was simply the legitimate Pope. The Council, as we have seen, called the good and murdered Archbishop of Constantinople, Flavian, a plant of the Vine, torn up by that wild beast the heretical Patriarch of Alexandria; but of Leo it is said that our Lord had made him the Guardian of the Vine. In these words then it recognizes not only St. Leo, but the whole line of Roman Pontiffs down to his time as ' Guardians of the Vine.' It puts the stamp of an œcumenical council upon the

* "Die orthodoxe katholische Anschauung im Gegensatz zum Papstthum und Jesuitismus, sowie zum Protestantismus. Nebst einem Rückblick auf die päpstliche Encyklica und den Syllabus vom 8. December 1864. Von J. J. Overbeck." Halle, 1865 (London: Williams & Norgate).—See p. 101—111.—Many subjects, which I could only touch upon in this book, are more fully treated in the German work, and vice versâ.

fact that Peter was first appointed by our Lord Guardian of the Vine, and that every Roman Pontiff succeeding him was appointed by our Lord as such. In no other way was St. Leo appointed by the Saviour the Guardian of the Vine but this." The very same Council which issued the famous Canon XXVIII. advocating the Roman Supremacy!? If one requires consistency in the words and dealings of every sensible person, one must do much more so with respect to the proceedings of an œcumenical council guided by the Holy Ghost. Now it is a hermeneutical rule that a controverted passage of an author is to be interpreted by other plain passages of the same. Well, the Canon XXVIII. is unmistakeably plain, is an impregnable bulwark against papal encroachments, and shows fully the consciousness of the Fathers that, opposite Rome, they must keep on the defensive or are sure to lose their position. From this feeling the necessity of the canon arose. We know that the Pope and the Romish Church did not approve of this canon. But what was to be done? No subsequent œcumenical council cancelled the canon, and it obtains up to this day its place in the Canon-law of the Eastern Church whether Orthodox or Papal. Why has not the Pope used his divine power (if the council knew such a thing) to abolish it? Now these very same Fathers call Pope Leo " the very person *intrusted by the Saviour with the Guardianship of the Vine.*" But *how* was he the Guardian of the Vine? The Vine was ravaged by the heterodox teaching of Eutyches, when our Saviour raised

CATHOLIC ORTHODOXY. 123

St. Leo to be the foremost champion of orthodoxy, and *thus* intrusted him *personally* with the Guardianship of the Vine, as He had intrusted St Cyril with the same Guardianship at the time of Nestorius, and St. Athanasius at the time of Arius. I think this interpretation is much more natural and congenial to the minds of the Fathers of Chalcedon. Unfortunately the chief argument of Mr. Allies' advocacy of Papal Supremacy rests on the wrong interpretation of the " Guardianship of the Vine."

But to return to Dr. Newman's faint outlines of primitive Papal Supremacy, I put down the passage, affixing to it a short Commentary :

Faint they (i. e. the ante-Nicene testimonies) may be one by one, but at least they are various, and are drawn from many times and countries, and thereby serve to illustrate each other and form a body of proof.

But if these testimonies turn out not to be to the point, or to be misunderstood or misinterpreted ?

Thus St. Clement, in the name of the Church of Rome, writes a letter to the Corinthians when they were without a bishop ;

This does not prove any pre-eminence of his see but, at most, St. Clement's personal influence and acquaintance with the Church of Corinth which he, having been St. Paul's fellow-labourer, must have known. Or are we to draw the inference from St. Polycarp's letter to the Philippians, that the see of Philippi was subject to that of Smyrna ? The Apostle St. John at Ephesus must have been too old at that time to be consulted in intricate quarrels, since in the last years of his life his bodily power seems to have been exhausted (Hieron.Comm.

in Ep. ad Galat. cp. 6). To the objection that in spite of the nearness of Smyrna and other celebrated Churches the Corinthians applied to distant Rome, I simply reply that the commerce between the capital and the chief towns of the empire must necessarily have been frequent. However, irrespectively of the distance, it appears to be most likely that St. Clement was personally known and respected in the Church of Corinth, and *therefore* his assistance requested; or if not personally known, he was consulted on account of his being a disciple of St. Paul, founder of the Church of Corinth. Abbé Guettée ("La Papauté schismatique," Paris, 1863, p. 30) remarks very appositely: "On ne peut inférer, ni de la lettre elle même, ni des circonstances dans lesquelles elle a été écrite, rien qui puisse faire considérer la démarche des Corinthiens comme une reconnaissance d'une autorité supérieure dans l'évêque ou dans l'église de Rome, ni la réponse comme un acte d'autorité. Les Corinthiens s'adressaient à une église où résidaient les collaborateurs de saint Paul, leur père dans la foi; et cette église, par l'organe de Clément, l'engageait à la paix et à la concorde, sans la plus légère prétention à une autorité quelconque." A. Archinard ("Les Origines de l'Église Romaine," tom. II. p. 148) finds also that the request of the Corinthians "constituait, non un appel proprement dit, mais une demande de médiation." A great many Roman divines do not mention this instance as a proof of the Roman Supremacy, led by the true feeling that one objectionable proof adduced is apt to injure the whole. Kenrick ("the Primacy of the Apostolic See vindicated." London, 1849, p. 131*seq.*) is rather timid in advancing this testimony: "The terms of the letter may not satisfy a fastidious critic that superior authority was claimed by the writer, because persuasion only is used; but the judicious reader will easily understand, that where passions are excited, they can scarcely be subdued by urging abstract views of power. The interposition of a distant prelate in the internal affairs of the Church of Corinth, *cannot be accounted for satisfactorily unless by reference to his universal charge.* [I think it is easier and more natural to account for it as we have done, without referring to the pretended charge.] ... Had not Clement felt it to be his duty, he scarcely would have ventured, in such circumstances, to address the revolters." [A strange sort of argument. Did St. Clement then obtrude himself on the Corinthians? Was he not asked? Would it not have been both unchristian and unpolite to refuse his mediation? There was nothing to venture in this case. Yea, even unasked he might have addressed authoritatively the revolters in the name of St. Paul, their and his common father in the faith.] And now hear the high strain of Pitzipios (" L'Église Orientale," Rome, 1855, I. Partie, p.43): "Du temps encore des Apôtres, les Corinthiens *soumirent à la décision du Pape* St. Clément leurs contestations, que celui-ci *régla* par une lettre aux Corinthiens." Finally, Mr. Allies ("The See of St. Peter," 3rd Edition, London, 1866, p. 154 *seq.*) says: "... the Bishop of Rome, and he alone, claims a control over the Churches of the whole world.... The well-known instances of S. Clement writing to the Church of Corinth to heal its divisions, in the very lifetime of S. John.... are *sufficient proofs* (! ?) of this. The force of the fact lies in this, that the Bishop of Rome, and he alone, *claims*, as need may arise, a control over all; but no one claims a control over him." However, St. Clement did not *claim* a control, but was asked. Now this argument is very poor indeed. One can scarcely believe that the same person wrote "The English Church cleared from the Charge of Schism," a book of stupendous learning and diligence, and "The See of St. Peter," full of bold assertions and weak proofs. Mr. Mouravieff ("Question religieuse d'Orient et d'Occident," 3ème livraison. St. Pétersbourg, 1859, p. 141) says of Mr. Allies: "Après avoir écrit un ouvrage très-étendu et savant contre la suprématie papale, lorsque, plus tard, il eut lui-même plié la tête sous le joug, il ne fut pas en état de réfuter, dans une brochure insignifiante, les preuves canoniques de son livre, basées sur les Conciles; aussi sa rétractation n'est-elle qu'une accusation de plus." Indeed, there is plenty of reason to quote *Allies versus Allies*. It would be a real benefit to every one, whether Anglican or Papist or Orthodox, if Mr. Allies would take upon himself the trouble *to refute, if he can, line by line his former substantial work*, and he ought to do so for his own conscience' sake, since his former work continues to attract and convince. His "Preface to the Third Edition: being a Letter to Dr. Pusey" (p. 1—64), does not supply this want.

> St. Ignatius of Antioch addresses the Roman Church, and it only out of the Churches to which he has written, as 'the Church which has the first seat in the place of the country of the Romans;'

St. Ignatius' letter to the Romans, although considered the first marked proof of Rome's supremacy, is rather *derogatory* to the papal claims. "Ignatius—to the Church.... which presides in the place of the district of the Romans.... which also presides in love ....." Thus the Bishop of Rome presides *within the district of the Romans,* as the Bishop of Alexandria does in Egypt, Libya, and Pentapolis, and as the Bishop of Antioch does within his territory (Cf. Canon VI. of the Council of Nice). Consequently Ignatius points to Rome being the head of the Western Patriarchate; not as if the Patriarchal system was, at such an early date, already nominally introduced, but our passage contains a real germ of what was fast developing. If St. Ignatius has wished to express the modern notion of Papal Supremacy, he would and ought to have written, " ἥτις καὶ προκάθηται τῆς καθολικῆς ἐκκλησίας." Möhler ("die Einheit in der Kirche," p. 207 note) understands the words of the Metropolitan Church Constitution. See "die orthod. kath. Anschauung," p. 106.

But as the Papal Supremacy cannot be realized from the former part of the sentence, the Roman champions (Möhler, Döllinger, Hefele, Rothensee,

Alzog, Wocher, &c.) try to elicit it from the latter part, translating ἀγάπη, "Liebesbund" (a society of persons loving each other), i. e. "the Church." How far English Catholics participate in this German Catholic forgery I do not know. Most certainly those who so translate cannot adduce a single instance of ἀγάπη signifying "a society." Such a society of loving friends would have been called ἑταιρεία. The several meanings of ἀγάπη are, 1. a fond affection (opp. ἔρως "carnal love"), 2. the love-feast of the Early Church, 3. the kiss of peace (Lat. pax or osculum pacis), 4. an extra allowance at table in convents (Lat. caritas, pitancia), 5. Alms, 6. a term of respect (Cf. Littledale's Glossary to his Offices of the Holy Eastern Church, 1863). Neither of these significations points to "Liebesbund," although Döllinger and Wocher attempt to derive it from "love-feast," Pichler ("Geschichte der kirchlichen Trennung zwischen dem Orient und Occident," 1844, tom. I., p. 105 note), however, disagrees, on this point, from his master Döllinger.—Again, had St. Ignatius wished to express by a word the Presidency of the Roman *Church*, he would rather have written "προκαθημένη τῆς πίστεως" instead of τῆς ἀγάπης. The longer Latin translation renders the words: "Ignatius— Ecclesiæ—fundatæ in dilectione;" the shorter: præsidens in caritate;" the first Syriac: "sedens in capite (i. e. præsidens) in caritate;" the second Syriac very freely: "— ecclesiæ — illuminatæ — amore Jesu Christi;" similarly both Armenian versions which were made from the Syriac. Thus:

"præsidens caritatis" means "caritate excellens," which is most apposite to what St. Ignatius wants to express. He entreats the Roman Christians not to exert themselves in his behalf, not to yield to their world-known affectionate feeling by taking steps for his liberation, and thus to deprive him of the crown of martyrdom.—And now, to sum up the evidence, we find that, even were the Pope's Presidency over the Catholic world, at these early times, an undoubted and established fact, this passage at least would not be available for the purpose. But how easy certain people take the matter, Bishop Kenrick (l. c. p. 101) shows, who, after having quoted the passage, simply and naïvely adds : "This language clearly indicates the pre-eminence of the Roman Church;" as if anybody, who accepts the holy canons, doubted it, but this pre-eminence has nothing to do with Supremacy, which Kenrick is anxious to establish.

St. Polycarp of Smyrna betakes himself to the Bishop of Rome on the question of Easter ;

"He *went*, it appears, to Rome, and the Pope, St. Anicetus, and he, not being able to agree as to the rule of keeping Easter, agreed to retain their several customs ; *a fact which is as much opposed to the present notion of the Roman Supremacy, as any fact can well be.*" Allies : " The Church of England cleared," 2nd edition, p. 20.

the heretic Marcion, excommunicated in Pontus, betakes himself to Rome ;

"Here it is sufficient to ask, which is the stronger proof, the flight of the profligate Marcion to Rome in behalf of the Supremacy, or the answer of the Roman clergy *in denial of it?*" Allies: " The Ch. of Eng." p. 71.—However, considering that Epiphanius is the only reporter of this incident; considering that his credulity was easily led away,* and that his dramatic description of this incident strongly savours of Fama's myth, no conscientious critic can admit so untenable a proof. Justin, Irenæus, Tertullian, Cyprian, Clemens Alex., the Author of the Φιλοσοφούμενα (Hippolytus?), Cyril of Jerusalem, Eusebius the Church-Historian, James of Nisibis, Ephrem Syrus, Jerome, Theodoret, the Armenian Bishop Esnig (5th Century), Philastrius (4th Century), Chronicon Edessenum (6th Century), &c., speak of Marcion, and some of them speak of him and his system at considerable length, but do not mention Marcion's appeal to Rome, either not knowing or not believing the tale, or attaching too little importance to the matter to touch upon it.

Soter, Bishop of Rome, sends alms, according to the custom of his Church, to the Churches throughout the Empire, and, in the words of Eusebius, " affectionately exhorted those who came to him, as a father his children";

I do not know what this has to do with Papal Supremacy, unless the Romans argue thus : The old practice of the popes " to do good to all the brethren in every way, and to send contributions to many churches in every city" (Eus. H. E. IV.

* J. Fessler, " Institutiones Patrologiæ," 1850, tom. I. p. 647 : " Leviores quidam nævi, *in rebus præsertim historicis* et chronologicis, ubi vir, fraudis ipse nescius pietatisque zelo æstuans, *nimia quandoque facilitate fidem adhibuit* . . . ."—R. A. Lipsius " Zur Quellenkritik des Epiphanios." 1865 Wien.

23), is the duty of a Superior, since the *right* of Supremacy involves the *duty* of Charity ("sollicitudo omnium ecclesiarum," Rothensee), and the discharge of a duty points to a right existing.—If the Romans conclude in this way, they would have to show first that the Popes considered this charity to be the duty involved in their Suprematial Office. Now, St. Dionysius does not alone not assign this reason as the origin of the practice, but simply and plainly derives it from *Pagan* Rome : "Thus .... you preserve, as Romans, the practices of your ancestors the Romans" (Eus. l. c.). Moreover, what is more natural than that the first and most important Bishop of Christendom should assist his brethren abroad. True, the Bishops of Rome were then not yet living in such an affluence of wealth as to be able to give banquets of more than royal splendour (Ammian. Marcellin. XXVII. 3), but they were not so poor that they could not easily give large contributions merely from the motive of charity. Euseb. (H. E. V. 21) informs us that about A. D. 180 "*many* of those eminent at Rome for their wealth and kindred, with their whole house and family" joined the Christian Church.*

That Soter " affectionately *exhorted* those who came to him, *as a father his children*," is what every one would expect from a *senex venerabilis* who is Bishop of the first Church of Christendom. But mark as well that Pope Victor was *reproved* by Polycrates, who finished his letter by the significa-

* Hippolytus (Refut. IX. 11) calls Pope Zephyrinus δωροληπτην καὶ φιλάργυρον.

tive words: "We ought to obey God rather than *men!*" (Eus. H. E. V. 24). Further on Eusebius says: "Upon this, Victor, the Bishop of the Church of Rome, forthwith endeavoured to cut off the churches of all Asia, together with the neighbouring churches, as heterodox, from the common unity. And he publishes abroad by letters, and proclaims, that all the brethren there are wholly excommunicated. But this was not the opinion of all the bishops. They immediately *exhorted* him, on the contrary, to contemplate the course calculated to promote peace, unity, and love to one another. Their writings too are extant, *very severely censuring* Victor. Among this also was Irenæus.... He becomingly also *admonishes* Victor, not to cut off whole churches of God, who observed the tradition of an ancient custom." Here you see pious Bishops *exhorting* a Pope, not only *claiming* but *exercising a control* over a Pope, and even *censuring* a Pope. How, then, can Mr. Allies ("The See of St. Peter," p. 155) assert: "The force of the fact lies in this, that the Bishop of Rome, and he alone, claims, as need may arise, a control over all; *but no one claims a control over him*"? On the contrary, Pope Anicetus and Bishop Polycarp only tried "*to persuade*" each other (Eus. H. E. V. 24).

But to return to the letter "ascribed" (Euseb.) to St. Dionysius of Corinth, and directed to Pope Soter, its testimony is rather doubtful, since Dionysius himself owns of his letters that "these the apostles of the devil have filled with tares, ex-

changing some things, and adding others" (Eus.
H. E. IV. 23).

the Montanists from Phrygia came to Rome to gain the countenance of its Bishop; Praxeas from Africa attempts the like, and for a while is successful;

The Montanists calculated very wisely that, if they could gain the countenance of the first Bishop of Christendom, they would get a greater ascendency than by any other means. Most likely they speculated at the same time on the passions of parties at the great court of the Pope. No doubt there were *côteries* and *intrigues* at such a court, and heretics could more easily find a court-party to lean upon by engaging themselves to combat the other. But was there not another reason in Rome to attract the Montanists? As early as the end of the first or the beginning of the second century we find in the Roman Church a party of rigorous principles, the exponent of which is the "Pastor" of Hermas. These principles, although indeed not Montanistic, prepared the ground for the later heresy. The times of persecution nurtured this rigorousness, raised the authority of Martyrs and Confessors, and fixed the eyes of pious Christians on the imminent coming of the Lord. Thus Rome was a fit place to be chosen as central point of Montanism. The Montanists transacted with the Popes, till at last "*literæ pacis*" were issued (*jam emissas*). Who was the Pope that issued those credentials of Church-communion? Either Eleutherus or Victor. I think (with Döllinger and Gieseler*) it is the latter. The stern and passionate Victor, excommunicating or threatening to excommunicate the Asian bishops, receives into Church-communion the Montanists who were excommunicated by those bishops. Victor was an African; and Africa was a prolific soil of rigorous sects rooted in the austerity of the national character. Thus Victor was not opposed to the rigorous tendency of Montanism; its excommunication by his Asian antagonists was rather a recommendation to him; and the peaceful words of the Confessors at Lyons and Vienne to Eleutherus in behalf of the Montanists may have had their influence on him. Thus the Church of Rome was *contaminated by heresy*, i. e. by Church-communion with heretics who were explicitly excommunicated by their ordinary bishops. It is true, the Pope rescinded the heretical bond, as he found he was deceived by the Montanists. But whether this imposition lasted an hour, or a year, or a century—it is clearly shown by our case that *the Pope is not a safe Guardian of the Vine*.

The person by whom Victor was disabused and induced to revoke his "literæ pacis" in favour of the Montanists, was Praxeas, once a Montanist himself; but at that time an inveterate enemy of the sect. He came to Rome chiefly for the purpose of having his enemies excommunicated. Of course, he addressed himself to the Pope, because it was

---

* Döllinger: Handbuch der christlichen Kirchengeschichte, I. p. 280; Gieseler: Lehrbuch der Kirchengeschichte, 4 edit., I. p. 287.— Neander, Schwegler, and A. Ritschl believe the Pope to be Eleutherus.

CATHOLIC ORTHODOXY. 135

the Pope who had received them into Church-communion. This is the plain and simple reason why he applied to the Pope; and there is not a jot in the whole relation which justifies the gratuitous supposition of those who point to Praxeas as recognizing the supreme power of jurisdiction lodged in the Pope. Praxeas not only attained his end, but succeeded in gaining over Pope Victor to his own heresy of Patripassianism (Cf. Tertull. de Præscript. cp. 53, and Kurtz : Handbuch der allgemeinen Kirchengeschichte, 3 edit. 1853, I. p. 275). Another proof that *the Pope is not a safe Guardian of the Vine.* And not only Victor but also his successors Zephyrinus and Callistus countenanced the heresy of Patripassianism or Monarchianism, as we know from the contemporary author (St. Hippolytus ?) of the Φιλοσοφούμενα.

St. Victor, Bishop of Rome, threatens to excommunicate the Asian Churches;

We heard already what Eusebius relates about the matter. Mark well ἀποτέμνειν πειρᾶται, "he *attempts* to cut off," but was restrained by his dissenting brother bishops, who checked him effectually, and censured his arrogance in condemning the observance of Apostolical practices, in order to create a uniformity in the Church. He made his position very awkward indeed, being obliged to withdraw what he so obstreperously began. The Romans are quite right in appealing to Victor as a fair specimen of a Pope holding (or, at least, affecting) Supremacy. Victor is indeed the first Pope who went beyond the limits of his lawful Primacy. His imperiousness led him to experiment on the Church-government, but his attempt to rule the Church absolutely proved to be a piteous miscarriage. The bishops disavowed the principles of Victor's administration as novel and uncatholic; and Victor was repeatedly defeated. Victor went his own way, and associated with all sorts of heterodox people. Victor's proceedings were branded as *innovations* and *usurpations*, and Victor was compelled to *yield*, thus recognizing himself that he did not claim an inalienable right (which he would have acted wrongly to resign), but affected an unlawful privilege. This affected privilege sprang from imperiousness, and imperiousness springs from the Original Sin, since the serpent said unto the woman: " Ye shall be as gods !" And imperiousness is most perfectly developed in Papal Supremacy. No wonder that Victor's principles were gradually developed by some of his successors; mankind would not be "fallen mankind," if it were otherwise. But what was considered Catholic at Victor's time, the self-same thing is Catholic up to the end. Polycrates resisted Victor's usurpation; and so did all the upholders of Catholic truth in the subsequent ages oppose the unlawful claims of Papacy. Mr. W. Palmer (Dissertations on subjects relating to the "Orthodox" or "Eastern Catholic" Communion, 1853, p. 105) remarks to the point: "That spirit of unbounded domination, with the capacity for exercising it, which characterized pagan Rome has been transmitted as a local inheritance to Rome Christian. Already in the second century a Pope (Victor) could think of cutting off from Communion whole Churches merely because they presumed to maintain a ritual tradition differing from his own : And a long history might be written of the encroachments, fresh precedents, conflicts, partial and occasional defeats, great and ultimate victories and conquests, by which the Roman See has subjugated and incorporated under its dominion the greater part of the Church, so as to afford a parallel with the gradual extension of the pagan Roman Empire over the habitable and civilized world." Dr. Newman accounts for this opposition by the tendency of fallen mankind to shake off the yoke of authority. I leave it to my readers to choose between the two ways, how to account for the Pope's Supremacy. I conclude with a passage of Mr. Allies " the Ch. of Engl. cleared," p. 59 : " Could Polycrates have acknowledged in the Roman See any authority different *in kind* from that of other Bishops, such as the Supremacy ? Could he have said distinctly to the power which could cut him off from the Church of God and the covenant of salvation, ' having conferred with my brethren throughout the world, ... I am not alarmed at what I am threatened with ' ? i. e. excommunication from Rome."

St. Irenæus speaks of Rome as "the greatest Church, the most ancient, the most conspicuous, and founded and established by Peter and Paul," appeals to its tradition, not in contrast, indeed, but in preference to that of other Churches, and declares that " in this Church every Church, that is, the faithful from every side, must meet" or "agree together, *propter potiorem principalitatem.*" "O Church, happy in its position," says Tertullian, "into which the Apostles poured out, together with their blood, their whole doctrine!"

First of all we have, in this eulogy of the Roman Church, not to *strain* the expressions, for panegyrical exaggerations are of daily occurrence. For instance, Dr. Newman knows as well as St. Irenæus knew, that Rome is *not* the most ancient Church, which is Jerusalem. And St. Iresænus knew, most likely, what Firmilian (writing in the name of the Asian Bishops) knew: "Eos, qui Romæ sunt, *non* ca in omnibus observare, quæ sint ab origine tradita, et *frustra Apostolorum auctoritatem prætendere.*"—Now let me give an explanation of the Irenæan *locus palmaris*, "this splendid testimony" (Kenrick) of Papal Supremacy, in the words of the Roman Catholic Dr. Pichler (Geschichte der kirchlichen Trennung zwischen dem Orient und Occident. 1864, I. p. 106 note 1): "On this passage, as well as on many others, there is too much stress laid. Irenæus produces the Roman Church alone to the heretics, not because the faith of every single Catholic Church had to conform to that of the Roman Church—which has neither been maintained by Irenæus nor by any one else for a long time—but because the true faith has been preserved in every Catholic Church through Apostolical tradition, and therefore necessarily so in the greatest and oldest Church, which was founded by the two chief Apostles, and, for that reason, had a prominent excellency."—Abbé Guettée (La Papauté schismatique, p. 39 *seq.*) justly remarks: "Comment saint

Irénée, qui s'applique à donner *la foi universelle* comme règle de la croyance particulière et qui s'étend précisément sur ce point dans le chapitre d'où le text ci-dessus est tiré, aurait-il pu *logiquement* dire ce que les papes et leurs théologiens lui attribuent ? Il eût alors ainsi raisonné : *Il est nécessaire* de prendre pour règle la croyance de toutes les Églises ; mais *il suffit* d'en appeler à celle de l'Église de Rome à laquelle on doit se rattacher et se soumettre à cause de sa primauté. Saint Irénée n'a pas émis une opinion aussi peu raisonnable. Il pose en principe la foi universelle comme règle ; et il indique la foi de l'Église de Rome comme vraie, grâce au concours des fidèles qui s'y rendaient de toutes parts et qui y *conservaient* ainsi la tradition apostolique. Comment la conservaient-ils ? Parce qu'ils auraient protesté contre tout changement aux traditions de leurs propres Églises dont ils étaient à Rome les témoins. Saint Irénée ne donne pas la prétendue autorité divine de l'évêque de Rome comme le principe de la conservation de la tradition dans l'Église de cette ville ; mais il attribue *logiquement* cette conservation aux fidèles des autres Églises qui contrôlaient ses traditions par celles de leurs propres Églises et qui formaient ainsi un obstacle invincible à toute innovation."—A. Ritschl ("Die Entstehung der altkatholischen Kirche," 2 edit. 1857, p. 573 *seq.*) says : " Vor Cyprian hat von den uns bekannten Schriftstellern nur Irenæus einen Vorrang der römischen Gemeinde vor allen übrigen behauptet : Ad hanc enim, &c." (He re-translates *potentiorem principalitatem* ἱκανωτέραν ἀρχαιότητα, which, I think, is not so correct as ἱκανωτέραν πρωτείαν (Thiersch), or ἐξαίρετον πρωτεῖον (Philaret, Metropolitan of Moscow, similarly Döllinger). Alzog renders ἱκανώτερον κῦρος, smuggling in the papal notion of "jurisdictional authority.") " Dem Zusammenhang nach ist damit nicht mehr gemeint, als dies, dass sich Irenæus benügen könne, die durch die bischöfliche Nachfolge vermittelte Ueberlieferung des Glaubens bloss in der römischen Gemeinde anstatt in allen Gemeinden nachzuweisen, weil wegen des hervorragenden Alters [?!] jener zu erwarten sei, dass die übrigen Gemeinden mit derselben übereinstimmen. *Auch durch diese Aussage wird es bewiesen, dass die Idee eines römischen Primats* [R. means "Supremacy"] *damals höchstens ein Anspruch auf die Zukunft, nicht aber ein festes altgegründetes Recht war.* Es ist der Charakter der Stufe der Katholischen Kirche, deren Entstehung geschildert werden sollte, dass sie den einträchtigen Episcopat als höchste Form der kirchlichen Verfassung gewonnen hat, während das drastischere Organ der Einheit, der Primat, im Bedürfnisse [?!], im Wunsch und im Ansprucho zu *keimen beginnt*, aber weder schon durch eine ausgebildete Theorie, noch durch folgerechtes Handeln der römischen Bischöfe nach einer solchen sich kund gibt." Now the reader himself may judge of the following pompous passage of Bishop Kenrick (p. 102) : " A better or more powerful principality is ascribed to this (i. e. the Roman) Church, since heavenly empire surpasses earthly dominion; and its influence in maintaining the integrity of Christian tradition is shown from the necessity of harmony between all the local churches and this ruling church." Kenrick, and many Roman Catholics with him, do not distinguish the significations of "*necesse est*" (ἀνάγκη ἐστίν) and "*oportet*" (δεῖ). The former signifies a physical necessity, "it cannot be otherwise," therefore often synonymous with "consentaneum est"; the latter, on the contrary, implies a moral obligation, "all the other churches *ought* to agree with the Roman." On this last misinterpretation is founded Mr. Palmer's intimation ("A Treatise on the Church," vol. II. part VII. ch. V. p. 502): "The necessity of resorting to the Roman Church arose from the principality or pre-eminence of that Church." Mr. Allies ("the Ch. of Engl. cleared," p. 61 *seq.*) understands the meaning of our passage better: "I suppose that the actions of St. Irenæus towards the Apostolic See of the West are a comment upon his words respecting it. . . . He really means what he says, and what his actions indicate, that the Bishop of Rome was first among his brethren: and he does not mean a totally different thing, which his words are quoted to prove, namely, that the Bishop of Rome stood in the same relation to him and to all the other Bishops of the world as he himself stood in to his own presbyters at Lyons. If he did mean this latter thing, he selected the strangest words to express it, and he exemplified it by the strangest actions which I can well conceive." I think Mr. Allies' inference from the actions of a person explaining his words is much more reasonable than Dr. Newman's opposite course, considering "St.

Cyprian's own doctrine more weighty than his act" ("Development," p. 24).

Now, what imparted this *potentior principalitas* to the Roman Church? It is its foundation by the two Apostle-princes Peter *and* Paul. St. Irenæus and St. Dionysius of Corinth know only of this *double* foundation, and Tertullian agrees with them in the passage above quoted. It is as if God clearly showed by this the amalgamation of the Christians from Jewry and Paganism into one Universal Church, which ought to be aloof from any Particularism. What St. Peter was wanting, even after his conversion (Gal. ii. 11 *seq.*) St. Paul supplied. Therefore St. Peter *and* St. Paul together consecrated Linus to be the *first* Bishop of Rome, for the Apostles had the whole world allotted as their bishopric, and were not confined to a particular See. St. Peter was co-operating with St. Paul, and not overruling him, in spite of Luke xxii. 32, which the Infallibilists interpret of the Pope's doctrinal Supremacy. The Fathers did not understand the passage in this way. Let us hear one instance. St. Cyril of Alexandria in his Commentary on St. Luke (translated from an ancient Syriac version by the Rev. R. Payne Smith, Professor of Divinity and Canon of Christ Church, Oxford, 1859, p. 676 *seq.*) says: "For, lest his impending fall should lead the disciple to desperation, as though he would be expelled from the glories of the apostleship, and his former following (of Christ) lose its reward, because of his proving unable to bear the fear of death, and denying Him, at once Christ fills him with good hope, and grants him the confident assurance that he shall be counted worthy of the promised blessings, and gather the fruit of steadfastness. For He says, ' And do thou also, when converted, strengthen thy brethren.' O what great and incomparable kindness! The disciple had not yet sickened with the malady of faithlessness, and already he has received the medicine of forgiveness : not yet had the sin been committed, and he receives pardon; not yet had he fallen, and the saving hand is held out; not yet had he faltered, and he is confirmed : for ' do thou, He says, when converted, strengthen thy brethren.' So to speak belongs to One Who pardons, and restores him again to apostolic powers." Philaret of Moscow ("Entretiens sur l'Orthodoxie de l'Église Orientale," traduit par Soudakoff. Paris, 1862, p. 95) explains to the effect : "Tu seras ébranlé dans ta foi en moi, et tu tomberas ; mais tu seras de nouveau converti à elle, et tu te releveras. Tâche alors de réparer ta faute, et par une ardente repentance, par une inébranlable confession de la vérité, donne un exemple salutaire à ceux qui chancellent dans la foi."

That Peter and Paul chose Rome, *the Capital of the world*, as the sphere of their combined action, is so natural, that we rather should wonder if it were otherwise. 1. Rome was *the largest city of the world*, having a population of about four millions, thus surpassing even modern London by a third. Was not the richest harvest to be expected in such a populous place ? 2. Rome might be called, at that time, a *Summary of all nationalities*, partly settled down as residents, partly visiting the city on business or for pleasure. These different nations heard of Christianity, and either brought themselves back its germ to their countries, or, if settled at Rome, they had their relations and acquaintances in their mother country with whom they communed on all the matters dear to their heart. Thus Rome was like a flower, the seed of which is carried away by the wind in all directions. The first sermon of St. Peter at Jerusalem was delivered before a similar Universal public. 3. Rome was also *the centre of human depravation*. Read Tacitus, Juvenal, Persius, Petronius—and a ghastly picture, worse than many a representation of Hell in some mediæval writers, will stare at you. Here Christianity could show its divine origin and saving power, and could realize a new creation. Where sin abounded, grace abounded still more.

This importance of the Roman Church justifies its Primacy. The Fathers and Councils, therefore, sometimes trace back this Primacy to Rome being the Capital of the Roman empire, sometimes to the foundation of the Roman Church by the two chiefs of the Apostles. In order to fully appreciate the basis of the Roman Primacy we ought to combine both reasons. At the same time we must not overlook a great drawback in the Roman character which could, and really did, jeopardize the Roman Primacy. I allude to the propensity of Pagan Rome to rule the world by her laws, and to settle and, so to say, to codify every question in a juridical way. To rule and give laws—was also the distinctive feature of Christian Rome, as soon as the Christian Pontiff entered (though perhaps unconsciously) upon the heritage of the Pagan Pontiff (Cf. "Die orthodoxe katholische Anschauung," p. 103). The continual Eastern opposition was a salutary breakwater to this pernicious stream of absolute ecclesiastical monarchy. Therefore Rome did not succeed, yea, did not even dare, up to the great schism, to have the Roman supremacy sanctioned as a dogma. This only was done, when the Western Patriarchate was cut off from the East. Why did Rome never before move and have its suprematial rights settled by holy canons? Was it not an instinctive feeling, that *ecclesiastical rights never can grow into divine privileges?* Therefore Rome went on, supple and engaging, adopting the opponent's standing-point where the opponent disclaimed Rome's pretensions. This we see in the case of Apiarius. Mr. Allies ("Dr. Pusey and the Ancient Church," p. 70—80) takes great pains "rightly to estimate it," i. e. to defend Papal Supremacy, but in doing so he entangles himself in principles which scarcely can be approved. He says (p. 78 *seq.*) : " But why does not the Pope at once appeal to his apostolic authority? Why does he cite canons of Councils, instead of his inherent right? *I think it was part of the prudence which has ever belonged to the Apostolic See to cite to men what they would with least feeling of personal offence acknowledge:* now the canons of Councils, as being the acts of Bishops, were their own acts. [This is scarcely the course of open sincerity, though I may not call it direct double-dealing. However of what use is it to make one yield on the ground of canons, if he ought to yield on the ground of Papal Supremacy? If he, after your victory over him, persist in his abhorrence of papal authority, your victory is only apparent. But if you think that having once gained him, you could work and practise him into your belief, then he really did not belong to you, when you received him. This would be an unpardonable "pia fraus."] The Holy See, being filled with consistent tradition from the very first, and having to impress this upon the whole Church, *took men as it found them; employed one argument here, another there: content sometimes to accept as the concession of a Council what it knew to be contained in its own charge of feeding the universal Church.* [Now, to accept as the concession of a Council what one knows he possesses already, is most certainly not upright, but direct double-dealing in order to entice the other party.] Now I admit, that to those who look at ecclesiastical history outside and by whom the Guardianship of the Vine intrusted by the Saviour to the Pope is not acknowledged, this long process of unifying and, as I should term it, consolidating the Church's power, carried on by the Holy See century after century, may appear an usurpation. [And an usurpation it was, since the fundamental Church Constitution (as we find it unmistakably in the first Christian centuries) was broad, comprising the whole body of the Episcopate. Thus Christ had not taught a Supremacy of St. Peter's successor in the Roman See, else no controversy could have arisen on this point. But had Christ intended such a Supremacy, to be sure, he would not have laid a foundation to be contracted and centralised afterwards. The very foundation of a fabric is a very bad object for development, after a building has already been erected upon it. With regard to the Guardianship of the Vine intrusted by the Saviour to the Pope, we have already seen above Mr. Allies' mistake. This Guardianship is the prism through which he sees and reads history. This Guardianship (as he understands it, not as the Fathers meant it) exploded, his whole system breaks down.] Such a one, not having the key in his mind, may even cry out, after detailing this very case of Apiarius, ' I cannot imagine how a Divine right can be constructed out of a series of successful encroachments.' (Allies, Ch. of Engl. p. 145)." [This key is Mr. Allies' preconceived notion of the Guardianship, which prevents him from being an impartial judge. The former Mr. Allies is perfectly right in the last quotation. If one may not look at ecclesiastical history *outside*, I wonder how Mr. Allies came ever *inside*. Or is it requisite and necessary, first to accept, on the word of man, the Papal Supremacy, and then to try to mould and interpret history accordingly ? *Rationabile* sit obsequium vestrum !]

The Presbyters of St. Dionysius, Bishop of Alexandria, complain of his doctrine to St. Dionysius of Rome ; the latter expostulates with him, and he explains. The Emperor Aurelian leaves ' to the Bishops of Italy and of Rome ' the decision whether or not Paul of Samosata shall be dispossessed of the see-house at Antioch ;

Dr. Neale (" A History of the Holy Eastern Church. The Patriarchate of Alexandria," Vol. I. p. 72 *seq.*) states the case of St. Dionysius of Alexandria as follows: " These [ambiguous] expressions of S. Dionysius occasioned no small controversy throughout Pentapolis. Some, who were entirely opposed to the doctrine of Sabellius, saw as much danger in that of Dionysius; and their zeal caused them to forget their charity.—Without writing to their own Patriarch [what they ought to have done, cf. S. Athanas. de Sentent. S. Dionysii, § 13], without considering that he might be able to explain or willing to retract that which they deemed heretical in his statements, they laid a formal complaint before S. Dionysius of Rome. . . . . . A Council, whether already assembled for some other cause, or convoked by the Pope to decide on this, condemned without hesitation the doctrine contained in, or deduced from, the extracts submitted to them. The Bishop of Rome wrote, in their name as well as in his own, to his namesake of Alexandria, informing him both of the charges made against him, and of the decision to which the Council of Rome had come. At the same time, perhaps to vindicate himself from the suspicion of holding an opposite error, the Pontiff himself composed a work against the Sabellians.—The Bishop of Alexandria, on the receipt of these missives, found himself put, as it were, on his trial, with Rome for his accuser, and the whole Church for his judge. That he, whose whole life had been one long struggle with heresy,—he, who could look back on the time *when he confirmed in the faith or dis-*

posed to unity the very Pontiff who now appeared as his opponent,—that he should thus be compelled to stand on his defence must have been a bitter task; and one *which a proud spirit would probably have refused,* even though he had thereby plunged the whole Church into an abyss of confusion. Not so Dionysius.—He had already, it appears, addressed a letter to the Bishop of Rome on the same subject; and more particularly in defence of his unwillingness to use the word Consubstantial. But he now, under the title of a Refutation and Apology, composed four books, or epistles (for they are indifferently called by both names) against the accusations of the Pentapolitans. He complains that his accusers quoted his words in so disjointed and arbitrary a manner, that they misrepresented his sense;— that they uniformly affixed to them the worst signification, and made him say things which he was far from intending.... This apology was considered satisfactory;—and the Bishop of Alexandria retained his reputation as *the first living Doctor of the Church.*" Let us make a few remarks on this: 1. It was against the canons to pass over any of the successive judicial instances. Now, either the Bishop of Rome supposed the Bishop of Alexandria had been resorted to before, or he knew this had not been the case, and nevertheless acceded to the immodiate appeal of the Egyptians. In the latter case Rome would have acted wrongly. As to the appeal, of course, it could from the second See of Christendom only be directed to the first, which was Rome. However, it was apparently not the power of the Pope as Supreme Judge that cut the knot, but the peaceful disposition of that holy man, Dionysius of Alexandria, whom St. Athanasius called, on account of both his learning and piety, *a Doctor of the Church.* 2. There is still another reason for an appeal of the Egyptians to Rome. The Churches of Rome and Alexandria entertained a particularly close union; either because Alexandria was, so to say, the link which joined the Eastern to the Western Church, or because Alexandria, in its political importance, was only second to Rome, towards which it naturally gravitated. This is also the deeper reason why Alexandria obtained the second Patriarchate, whereas on ecclesiastical grounds, Antioch could claim a preference, for Alexandria was not a *direct* Apostolical See. Here again we see, how necessarily the political importance of a place must greatly influence its ecclesiastical standing. The two *Popes* (for both bore this title since time immemorial, and bear it up to the present day) were generally good friends. The Bishop of Alexandria calls that of Rome "*brother,*" and does not think to interfere with Rome's authority in addressing a letter "*to the faithful at Rome in general,* dwelling on the virtue of penitence, as effecting a re-admission into the Church even for apostates, and exhorting all parties concerned to peace and brotherly love" (Dr. Neale, l. c. p. 49 *seq.*). In the question of re-baptism "it would seem that [Pope] Stephen himself was the first to bring the subject before Dionysius. The latter, in his reply, earnestly requested the

Pope to proceed with moderation, and not to disturb the peace of the Church .... by any harsh decision with respect to the African and Oriental Prelates..... To S. Sixtus, the successor of Stephen, Dionysius again wrote; and a second time *urged* the necessity of union and mutual forbearance" (Dr. Neale, l. c. p. 60 *seq.*). It seems to have been an old custom,—and it lies in the nature of the thing—that the second See (Alexandria) appealed to the first (Rome), and the third (Antioch) to the second, as we find in the case of Paul of Samosata. This heretic was excommunicated by a Council of Eastern Bishops, to which the Bishop of Alexandria was summoned, but *not* the Bishop of Rome. The Council informs the Bishop of Rome of their sentence on Paul, however they do not submit this sentence to his approval or reconsideration. Paul would not yield, and the case was brought before the heathen Emperor Aurelian. What would have been more natural than that the pagan, who was certainly not versed in canon-law, referred the matter to the Bishop of the capital? And could any inference in favour of Papal Supremacy have been reasonably drawn from such a proceeding? But Aurelian did not even do such a thing, but left the decision "to the Bishops of Italy *and* of Rome." Abbé Guettée ("La Papauté Schismatique," p. 66 *seq.*) puts another side of the case in the foreground: "On a voulu voir dans la décision d'Aurélien une preuve en faveur de la juridiction universelle de l'évêque de Rome. Il est plus exact de dire que l'empereur voulut s'en rapporter, dans l'affaire qui lui était déférée, au témoignage d'évêques que les deux partis ne pouvaient raisonnablement récuser, puisqu'ils n'avaient aucun intérêt à favoriser l'un plutôt que l'autre ; d'évêques dont lui-même pouvait connaître facilement la sentence, puis qu'il demeurait au milieu d'eux. Il est à remarquer que l'empereur ne donna point la sentence de l'évêque de Rome comme irréfragable ; il le nomma avec les autres évêques d'Italie et *après eux ;* s'il le mentionna d'une manière spéciale, ce ne fut évidemment qu'à cause de l'importance de son siége fixé dans la capitale de l'empire, et non parcequ'il jouissait d'une autorité particulière. Il faut vraiment avoir grand besoin de *preuves* en faveur de la suprématie romaine pour en aller chercher dans la conduite d'un empereur païen, lorsque tous les détails ecclesiastiques de l'affaire de Paul de Samosate prouvent que cette suprématie n'était point reconnue par l'Église."—The Roman Catholic church-historian, Dr. Pichler ("Geschichte der kirchlichen Trennung zwischen dem Orient und Occident," I. p. 109), points to "the jurisdictional importance of Rome, *being the last instance in deciding doubtful civil cases*, in accordance with which already heathen Emperors, e. g. Aurelian in the case of Paul of Samosata, assigned the judgment on ecclesiastical affairs also to the Bishop of Rome [i. e. Rome was made a court of final appeal in ecclesiastical affairs, because it was, and had been for a long time, such a one in civil affairs]. Rothensee (who most anxiously sweeps together all historical dust which might be utilized for supporting the Papal Rock, and who is most thankful for every contribution, however small and insignificant, even for bad coin) calls Aurelian's proceedings "ein eclatantes historisches Zeugniss" in favour of Papal Supremacy. He refers to Bossuet ("Discours sur l'hist. univ.") who meant, that Aurelian had always seen that Christendom was kept together by its communion with the Pope, and, therefore, had commissioned the latter to decide in this case as well.—Here one cannot even say: "*Se non è vero, è ben trovato;*" for if heathen eyes saw so distinctly what Christian eyes could not see for centuries to come, either heathen penetration was unprecedented, or Christian stupidity unparalleled. Rothensee puts the very mockery of Leo of Acrida down as a testimony, and winds up his account by Bercastel's ("Geschichte der Kirche," II. 198) high words: "So weltkundig war es, dass man keinen bessern Beweis des wahren Christenthums haben konnte, als die Einigkeit mit der römischen Kirche. Paulus [von Samosata] wurde schändlich vertrieben, und Domnus kam an seine Stelle." Forsooth, it must be a desperate cause, where such untenable proofs are eagerly picked up and held out with triumphant joy!

But to return to St. Dionysius, we conclude with an observation of Dr. Neale (l. c. p. 84): "We may remark, as an instance of *the extraordinary power of the See of Alexandria*, that S. Dionysius, though writing to a Bishop [Basilides], addresses him by the title of *Son*,—an appellation not used in the like sense, *even by Rome.*" Dr. Newman can only state that Pope Soter "affectionately exhorted those who came to him, as a father his children;" but Eusebius does not mention a Bishop, whom Soter or another Pope called his Son.

St. Cyprian speaks of Rome as "the See of Peter and the principal Church, whence the unity of the priesthood took its rise—whose faith has been commended by the Apostles, to whom faithlessness can have no access;" St. Stephen refuses to receive St. Cyprian's deputation, and separates himself from various Churches of the East; Fortunatus and Felix, deposed by St. Cyprian, have recourse to Rome; Basilides deposed in Spain, betakes himself to Rome, and gains the ear of St. Stephen.

Before considering the testimony of St. Cyprian in favour of Papal Supremacy, the reader will allow me to make a preliminary remark.

It is a great drawback to attaining the truth of any historical fact or statement, when the sources are troubled. This is a sad experience which every patristic student, who does not, in company with the great public, swim on the surface of the "textus recepti," is obliged to undergo. We have already heard St. Dionysius of Corinth complaining of the corruption of his writings which "the apostles of the devil have filled with tares, exchanging some things, and adding others, for whom there is a woe reserved." Dr. Cumming ("Tractarianism and Popery," 3rd edit. p. 85 *seq.*) says: "The corruptions of the writings of the Fathers is a topic I must not pass over. Erasmus says in his Epistles (In S. Basilii librum de Spiritu Sancto),—' I appeared to myself to have detected, in this work, what we behold with indignation to have been done in certain of the most celebrated and extolled writers, as in Athanasius, Chrysostom, and Jerome. You ask, what is this? After I had gone through half of the work without weariness, the phraseology appeared to me to belong to another parent, and to breathe a different genius; sometimes the diction swelled out to the tragic style, and it subsided again into common discourse; sometimes it appeared to me to have something flowing softly. .... From these circumstances a suspicion entered my mind, that some student, in order to render the volume more copious, had interwoven some things, either grafts culled from other authors (for this subject has been accurately handled by many of the Greeks), or devised by himself; for some of these are erudite, but differing from Basil's style. .... Moreover, it is a most wicked species of contamination, to interweave one's own cloth with most distinguished purple of celebrated men, or, to express myself more correctly, to corrupt their generous wine with one's own dead stuff; which has been done, with intolerable sacrilege, in the divine Jerome's Commentaries on the Psalms, so evidently, that it cannot be denied.' And, again, quoting still from Erasmus (In Hilarium Epist. lib. 28),—'What is this temerity with other people's books, especially those of the ancients, whose memory is (or ought to be) sacred to us ... that every one, according to his fancy, should shave, expunge, add, take away, change, substitute?' And, once more (In Athanas. Ep. ad Serapionem, de Spiritu Sancto), —'We have given some fragments of this sort;

for what purpose? you will say: that it may hence appear with what impiety the Greek scribes have raged against the monuments of such men, in which even to change a syllable is sacrilege. And what has not the same temerity dared to do among the Latins, in substituting, mutilating, increasing, and contaminating the commentaries of the orthodox?' A multitude of works, it seems, have been falsely ascribed to Chrysostom. In the Benedictine edition of that Father, tom. V. p. 672 (Paris, 1836), in the admonition to the homily on the 15th Psalm, we read—'John Chrysostom was so highly esteemed by the Greeks, that his works and small treatises were sought with the greatest eagerness; and whatever bore the name of Chrysostom was held as genuine by men not endowed with critical knowledge, such as were almost all those of the later ages. These were persons who rashly embellished with the name of Chrysostom sermons and homilies written by themselves. Transcribers of books also, for the sake of gain, sold homilies patched together by themselves or others, with the name of Chrysostom in the title page. Hence proceeded innumerable spurious works, of which some immediately supply the evidences of spuriousness; others require a full investigation.' Doubts, also, are felt about Basil's works, as may be seen by the Benedictine Preface (Paris, 1721). 'It remained that I should separate the true works of Basil from the false ones; which separation revealed a labour of the most extensive kind, since there are not a few of his writings that are called in question, but *all* of them. The learned, indeed, differ among themselves respecting the number of the homilies on "the six days' work" and the Psalms. These 31 Orations are not all ascribed to one and the same writer. The two books which we have on Baptism are held to be doubtful by some persons. The book on true Virginity is controverted. That most ample book on the first 16 chapters of Isaiah is not exempt from all suspicion. The opinion of all persons is not one respecting the five books against Eunomius. There are those who have not been ashamed to place among the false and supposititious, the last 15 chapters, and those the principal chapters, of the book on the Holy Spirit. The opinions of the ancients and more modern concerning his ascetic writings do not agree. Hardly anything certain can be defined respecting the Liturgy. His Epistles contain, as it were, a sort of seminary of quarrels and discords. For, in what year, in what month, from whom to whom, respecting what subject, they were written, is daily, vehemently, and sharply disputed. All must perceive, I think, how easy it is to err in this so great variety of things and opinions as in a moonless night.' Of the falsifications of the works of the Fathers generally, we read in the same Preface—'It is difficult to say how great diligence must be applied by him, who wishes certainly and safely to decide respecting the spuriousness or genuineness of any work; for it is wonderful, since truth and falsehood so greatly differ, yet one very frequently so much resembles the other, that in distinguishing between them, we can scarcely avoid error, unless we take great care.' And again : 'Perhaps there is no class of men, who have more injured good study, than those who have mixed up the true writings of the Fathers with false ones. For how many evils have, both formerly and in the present day, sprung up from hence, every one who is not altogether unexperienced in ecclesiastical matters, fully knows; *doctrines are obscured, morals are polluted, history falters, tradition is disturbed;* and to express my meaning in a word, if once the genuine writings of the holy Fathers are confounded with the adulterous ones, all things must necessarily be confounded together. The examples of what I have stated are too frequent for it to be necessary for me to mention any of them. I will only call to mind the imprudence of the Apollinarists and the Eutychians, who, when they had promulgated their own works for the sincere and true writings of the holy Fathers, so infected the whole Church, that even until this present day it has been impossible to close and cure this kind of wound. For, at the present day, so great is the disagreement among the erudite respecting the authorship of certain writers, that if any one adduces any evidence either of that great Athanasius, Bishop of Alexandria, or of Julius, the high Pontiff, or of Gregory the wonder-worker, immediately you will hear some say that Athanasius, Julius, Gregory, did not say these things, but Apollinarius, some of whose works were formerly deceitfully attributed to those great men, in order that the more simple might be led astray. But, to be now silent respecting the Apollinarists and Eutychians, I will generally observe, that innumerable inconveniences flowed from the same fountain.'" Of what use was all the evidence drawn from the Apostolic Father, St. Ignatius of Antioch, up to the year 1644, since before that time only the interpolated and spurious works were known? How many of the Greek works of S. Ephræm Syrus, which I. S. Assemani published, might, on closer examination, prove to be spurious or falsified, since Ephræm's Greek "Testament" is so signally different from the Syriac original?

Perhaps the worst treatment, or at least a very bad one, was experienced by *St. Cyprian's works* by all sorts of corruption, both accidental and intentional, so that he who inquires into the views of that great man, ought to be cautious, lest he be deceived by a corrupt or forged text.* Jo. Georg. Krabinger, a

* Nectarius, Patriarch of Jerusalem, and Mouravieff charge the Roman Catholics with falsifying the texts of the Fathers, and Adam Zörnikaw in his classical work on the Procession of the Holy Ghost substantiates this charge by singling out and examining a lot of texts. In the second and third of his nineteen treatises he points out 25 falsifications in the Greek Fathers, and 43 in the Latin; but as the Latin forgeries are too numerous, he treats them under the heading: "Corruptelæ variæ de ingenti numero unico argumento demonstrantur," p. 98—309. See Dr. Pichler in his remarkable work on the Schism between the East and the West (tom. I. p. 29 *seq.* note) where he touches upon Zörnikaw's work "*das leider* noch immer keinen lateinischen Kritiker gefunden hat," and most likely will not find, since it was published in the year 1774. If the Romans had found the Orthodox critic exceptionable, they would have replied long ago, whereas they now try "*es todtzuschweigen*," which is a common knack with them in such cases of perplexity. W. Palmer (" Dissertations on the Orthodox

most conscientious and felicitous Roman Catholic critic and last editor of Cyprian's works " *de catholicæ ecclesiæ unitate, de lapsis, et de habitu virginum* " (Tubingæ, 1853), remarks in the Preface to his minutely accurate edition : " Cypriani ... opera .... in omnibus, quotquot hucusque in lucem prodierunt, exemplaribus etiam post doctissimorum virorum curas hic illic *mirifice esse depravata atque interpolata* nemo nescit, qui aliquid in illis emendandis studii collocavit." I only notice a few instances, and those respecting the Roman primacy, putting in brackets the interpolations. *De Cath. Eccl. Unitate*, cp. 3 (Krabinger, l. c. p. 10 *seq.*): " Hoc erant utique et ceteri apostoli, quod fuit Petrus, pari consortio præditi et honoris et potestatis, sed exordium ab unitate proficiscitur [*et Primatus Petro datur*], ut ecclesia Christi una [*et cathedra una*] monstretur. [*Et pastores sunt omnes, sed grex unus ostenditur, qui ab apostolis omnibus unanimi consensione pascatur.*"] Compare Krabinger's elaborate critical note to the passage. But though the critic has, in this passage, incontestably cleared the way, theologians still continue quoting what Cyprian never wrote, e. g. Magon (" Handbuch der Patrologie und der kirchlichen Literaturgeschichte," 1864,

Communion," 1853, p. 147) says : "The general practice of Roman Catholic writers has been to defend all the existing doctrines of their Church, and (on the most important points) her discipline also and ritual, on the ground of tradition, either written or oral, preserved uninterruptedly from the beginning. Enslaved to this theory, *they have too often interpolated and corrupted the text of ancient authors, denied or explained away their plain meaning, and given a false colouring to Ecclesiastical history.*"

tom. I. p. 234). Döllinger and Möhler did mention the critical difficulty, it is true, but did not positively reject the *appendicula* or *glossema*, as Mr. Allies, very justly, did ("The See of St. Peter," 3rd edit. p. 180).—*De Cath. Eccl. Unitate*, cp. 4 : " Hanc ecclesiæ [*Petri*] unitatem qui non tenet, tenere se fidem credit ; qui ecclesiæ renititur et resistit [*qui cathedram Petri, super quam* (alii : *quem*) *fundata est ecclesia, deserit*], in ecclesia se esse confidit, &c."— Again, how early corruption crept into St. Cyprian's writings, we may infer from *Pope Pelagius II.* (in the sixth century) quoting the former passage in its interpolated form, and *Ivo* (Decret. de Sublimit. Episcop.) who quotes the latter.—We dispense with examining other Cyprianic texts, but point to the upwards of *twenty* spurious works attributed to Cyprian, in which Roman Primacy is often touched upon, and assuredly not without a desire of promoting its growth.

St. Cyprian is the first Father who not only lays a particular stress on the Roman Primacy, but has also wrought it out systematically, assigning to it a proper place in his theory of the Church, i. e. declaring it to be the crowning of the whole fabric. He philosophizes, as it were, on the component parts of the Church, and endeavours to find out their mutual relation, their office and sphere of activity, and shows how their co-operation constitutes the living organism of the Church. *Unity* is the great characteristic mark of the Church in spite of her diversified working. The *Representative* of this Unity is the Bishop of Rome.— St. Cyprian's expressions, warm and exaggerated, as one must expect from the hot temper of an African, seem sometimes to border on Roman Supremacy, but, on closer inspection, this appearance vanishes, and St. Cyprian ranks rather with the great upholders of true Primacy against the encroachments of Papal Supremacy. Words are to be interpreted by actions; and one's own doctrine is not more weighty than one's own act (as Dr. Newman thinks: "Development," p. 24). Still St. Cyprian's doctrine did not contradict his action, as the Romans fancy, but his action did only illustrate his doctrine, and gave a clue to it. The Romans, determined to find the Papal Supremacy in Cyprian's words, can, of course, find a contradiction between his teaching and his action, and thus devise an historical duality of a person who acted as he taught, and taught as he acted. Only Orthodoxy can understand and appreciate Cyprian, i. e. the *whole* Cyprian, without tearing him to pieces. And as such, as a living historical person (not as a lifeless and distorted letter, not as a mysterious sphinx-like hieroglyph), we venerate St. Cyprian; and we find that he is a defender of the true Primacy in the Catholic Church. Let us, therefore, insert a few words on

THE ORTHODOX NOTION OF THE LAWFUL PRIMACY IN THE CATHOLIC CHURCH.

JESUS CHRIST is the only foundation of the Catholic Church; the Apostles and the Bishops, their successors, are its pillars. The Congregation of the

Bishops constitutes the doctrinal authority of the Church; and the Bishops, meeting in an œcumenical Council, are, although *singly* fallible, *collectively* infallible judges of the faith, being led by the Spirit of Truth proceeding from the Father and sent by the Son, who is the head of the Church.

Thus the Unity of the Church rests on Jesus Christ, the one never-dying Head of the Church, who keeps together in the bond of Unity the body of the Bishops, who teach and rule the flocks of the faithful committed to their care. Now the head of the Church being invisible, its visible government by the Bishops may be called *aristocratic*.

All the Bishops enjoy the same honour and power; but as one Church surpasses another in importance, either for its apostolical foundation or for its political prominency, the Bishop of that Church has a higher station than his brother-bishops who govern Churches of an inferior importance. The *essential* power is in both the same, but the *accidental* influence of the one became greater than of the other. In this way were raised, with the consent and co-operation of the whole Church represented by œcumenical councils, five heads, viz. the Bishops of Rome, Constantinople, Alexandria, Antioch, and Jerusalem, called Patriarchs. Thus the aristocratical government grew into an *oligarchy*.

Every power, every government, naturally tends to *centralisation*. Already old Homer says: "Εἷς κοίρανος ἔστω!" The five patriarchs ranked according to the importance of their Sees. This we see most clearly from the Patriarch of Alexandria having, for a long time, the second place, and that of Antioch the third, although Antioch was founded *directly* by an Apostle, and Alexandria only *indirectly*. Again, Constantinople, though not even an Apostolical See, obtained the second place, because it was the second capital of the Roman Empire. In the same way Rome held the first place, being the capital of the world and founded by the two chiefs of the Apostles. The 28th Canon of the Council of Chalcedon plainly and unmistakeably states that the Fathers of the Council " *thought it fair to give the precedence* " (εἰκότως ἀποδεδώκασι τὰ πρεσβεῖα) to Rome, " BECAUSE *that city was the ruling one* " (διὰ τὸ βασιλεύειν τὴν πόλιν ἐκείνην). Now the Romans try to invalidate this Canon in two ways : 1. By affixing the meaning to it that here the Council only spoke of Rome as a Patriarchate, independently of Supremacy. But had Rome really held the Supremacy, the Fathers would have framed the Canon accordingly, or at least they would have alluded to it as naturally including the precedence. However, they accorded to Constantinople even τὰ ἴσα πρεσβεῖα, though the second place ; 2. The Romans reject the decree of the Fathers as being unlawful and never acknowledged by the Pope—thus allowing that it treated on the Primacy generally, and not merely on a matter of Patriarchal ceremony. But now fancy a congregation of Bishops so numerous as to constitute an œcumenical Council, and *all these Fathers* are ignorant of the Roman Supremacy ! *All* of them did not know anything like a Catholic tradition respecting the Roman

Supremacy! Apply here the rule of Vincent of Lerins: "*Quod semper; quod ubique; quod ab omnibus.*" The Church conferred the Primacy on the Bishop of Rome, which it never could have done, if this Primacy had been *divino jure*, i. e. Supremacy. Pope Zosimus, the successor of Innocent I., says expressly (Ep. II. ad Episc. Afr.): "Apostolicæ sedis auctoritati *patrum decreta* peculiarem quandam sanxere reverentiam." Thus the Bishop of Rome (*as long as true to his mission and to the Catholic faith*) was—

1. *The Head* (τὸ κάρα) of the Church, i. e. the first and most prominent of the Bishops. He is not called the Head (ἡ κεφαλὴ) of the Church in the meaning in which Christ is called so, nor as the visible deputy of the invisible Head, but simply as *the chieftain of the Bishops, who takes the lead*, St. Basil says: " . . . . while there is ruling the one head and, in truth, *the only head*, which is Christ." (Κρατούσης . . . τῆς μιᾶς καὶ μόνης ἀληθῶς κεφαλῆς, ἥτις ἐστὶν ὁ Χριστός.) St. Gregor. Naz.: "One Christ, one head of the Church." (Εἷς Χριστὸς μία κεφαλὴ τῆς ἐκκλησίας.) See *Macaire*, Evêque de Charkoff: "Théologie dogmatique Orthodoxe," Paris, 1860, tom. II. p. 271 *seq.*—The See of the Ecclesiastical Head enjoys the Presidency (προεδρία), as we read in the Office of the Orthodox Church on the 18th of February (Festum S. Leonis). The *Pedalion* calls the five Patriarchs Κάρας,* consequently the name

---

* With the ancient Greeks κάρα was an indeclinable noun of the neuter gender. The modern Greeks made it a declinable noun of the feminine gender.

of the Roman President would be Κάρα Καρῶν (Oberhaupt).

2. A Primacy in the Church was needed in order to *represent Unity*. In this quality of Representative the Pope had to take cognizance of what disturbed the peace of the Church. In this respect an appeal to him (after having gone through the due course of instances) was *lawful and final*, in case the Bishops gave their implicit or explicit assent to the sentence. If they did not agree, the cause was to be brought before a Council. In this way the Unity of the priesthood was bound to a *Centre,* that it might be preserved from Schism. St. Jerome (adv. Jovinian. lib. I.) : "At dicis : super Petrum fundatur ecclesia, licet id ipsum in alio loco super omnes apostolos fiat, et cuncti claves regni cœlorum accipiant, et ex æquo super eos fortitudo ecclesiæ solidetur, tamen *propterea unus eligitur, ut capite constituto schismatis tollatur occasio.*" And that this centre is not *absolute*, but ought to be in connection with the other Apostolical Sees, St. Augustine declares, of whom Pope Pelagius I. (Mansi IX. 716) says that he "dominicæ sententiæ memor, qua fundamentum ecclesiæ *in apostolicis sedibus* collocavit" taught : " In schismate esse, quicunque se a præsulum *earundem sedium* auctoritate vel communione suspenderit ; nec aliam esse ecclesiam, nisi quæ in pontificibus *apostolicarum sedium* est solidata radicibus." And this is also the view of Pope Pelagius himself (Mansi IX. 732) : "Quotiens dubitatio nascitur . . . ad apostolicas sedes pro recipienda ratione conveniant . . . . *Quisquis ergo Apostolicis divisus est sedibus, in schismate eum*

CATHOLIC ORTHODOXY. 167

esse non dubium est." By this the present Roman Papacy is condemned, being separated from all the other Apostolical Sees.

3. Every Bishop is a *Vicar of Christ*. St. Ambrosius (Comment. in Epist. 1 ad Corinth.) : " Episcopus personam habet Christi ; Vicarius Domini est." And the Primate is eminently a Vicar of Christ, because he has to represent the whole Church, and has to bear this great responsibility. But he is in no other sense Vicar of Christ than any other Bishop. He is, therefore, *not a Substitute of Christ, the invisible Head of the Church, and, consequently, does not possess any special powers or prerogatives derived therefrom.*

4. The Roman Primate, by a natural temptation of his great power and authority, tried to conquer privilege after privilege, and to extend his dominion at the expense of the episcopal rights. For this we do not blame him more than the other Patriarchs, who did the same, whenever they found a favourable opportunity. But, in order to preserve their privileges, the Roman Pontiffs looked for a basis which might render these privileges unattackable and inalienable. This basis they formed by tracing back Primacy to the Gospel and making it a *divine institution*. On this principle the Popes acted for a long time, but did not declare it a matter of faith. Consequently the Church, though protesting when the principle was brought forward, considered this opinion as personal and individual. But when the wrong principle of Supremacy was to be intruded upon the Church, the East

resisted to a man, and *cut off the faithless Primate,* " *the unjust steward;*" for " Consuetudo sine veritate, *vetustas erroris est.*" (St. Cyprian) —The West, trained, as it were, and prepared by its Patriarch, was easily dragged into the schism, since it had been practised upon by the Popes for centuries in this direction, whereas these, most wisely or rather cunningly, left the East alone, which was not so *tractable.*

5. After the Pope of Rome had forfeited his high position, *the second in rank, viz. the Patriarch of Constantinople, naturally took his place, and holds the Primacy in the Church till the Pope should abjure his errors and return to the Catholic fold.* Pedalion : " But since the first (Patriarch) fell away, that of Constantinople was left as the first." ('Επειδὴ δὲ ὁ πρῶτος ἀφηνίασεν, ἔμεινε πρῶτος ὁ Κωνσταντινουπόλεως.) The Patriarch of Constantinople possesses and exercises all the Primatial rights specified above ; and if he cannot and does not vie with the Pope, it is simply because he does not claim such extensive powers as the Pope usurps. The Pope is an *absolute Monarch;* the Patriarch of Constantinople is—what the Pope was and ought to have continued being— (to use a modern expression) a *constitutional Monarch,* and his government is monarchical, oligarchical, and aristocratical all at once.

But to return to St. Cyprian, I select the chief passage in favour of Roman Primacy, a passage

which was written at a time when he lived in peace
with Rome. I give Mr. Allies' translation, which
is on the whole correct, and leave to the judgment
of the reader to decide, whether St. Cyprian held
the Orthodox or the Romish notion of the Primacy.
The passage comprises the third and fourth chapters of "De Cath. Eccl. Unitate."

"This will be" (that is, falling away from the
Church into heresy and schism), "most dear brethren, so long as there is no regard to the source
of truth, no looking to the head, nor keeping to
the doctrine of our Heavenly Master [the 'source
of truth' and 'the head' are obviously the same
as the 'Heavenly Master']. If any one consider
and weigh this, he will not need length of comment or argument. It is easy to offer proofs to a
faithful mind, because in that case the truth may
be quickly stated. ['Probatio est ad fidem facilis
compendio veritatis' rather too freely translated.]
The Lord saith unto Peter: 'I say unto thee,' saith
He, 'that thou art Peter,' &c. To him again, after
His resurrection, He says, 'Feed My sheep.' Upon
one [Allies: 'Upon him, being one,' translates
'super *illum* unum,' which reading, though the *lectio
vulgata*, is critically not tenable] He builds His
Church; and though He gives to all the Apostles *an equal power*, and says, 'As my Father hath
sent Me, even so I send you, &c.; yet *in order to manifest unity* He has, by His own authority, so placed
the source of the same unity as to begin from one.
*Certainly the other apostles also were what Peter was,
endued with an* EQUAL *fellowship both of honour and*

power; but a commencement is made from unity, that the Church may be set before us as one .... He who holds not this unity of the Church, does he think that he holds the faith? He who strives against and resists the Church, is he assured that he is in the Church? For the blessed Apostle Paul teaches this same thing, and manifests the sacrament of unity, thus speaking: 'There is one Body and one Spirit, even as ye are called in one hope of your calling; one Lord, one Faith, one Baptism, one God.' This unity firmly should we hold and maintain, especially we Bishops presiding in the Church, in order that we may approve the Episcopate itself to be one and undivided. [This unity firmly should have held and maintained the Pope, and more firmly still than any other Bishop, since he was the chief and representative of the Unity in the Church, but he broke the bond, and thus divided the Episcopate. All that St. Cyprian says on the unity of the Church in the rest of this passage, and in the rest of his book, is spoken generally without the slightest allusion to the Bishop of Rome as the representative of unity, as every unprejudiced reader must see.] Let no one deceive the Brotherhood by falsehood; no one corrupt the truth of our faith by a faithless treachery. *The Episcopate is one, of which a part is held by each without division of the whole.* [Now the Pope made a division of the whole, rent the one Episcopate asunder, and he, the author of division—should be the Representative of Unity? As long as the Pope and the Episcopate 'dwelt together in unity,' the

Pope fulfilled his mission, but when he began to scatter the sheep, he incurred the sentence of St. Peter, 'He was numbered with us, and had obtained part of this ministry .... (but) let his habitation be desolate, and let no man dwell therein: and his bishopric let another take.'] The Church too is one, though she be spread abroad, and multiplies with the increase of her progeny. Even as the sun has rays many, yet one light; and the tree boughs many, yet its strength is one, seated in the deep-lodged root; and as when many streams flow down from one source, though a multiplicity of waters seem to be diffused from its broad overflowing abundance, unity is preserved in the source itself. Part a ray of the sun from its orb, and its unity forbids this division of light; break a branch from the tree, once broken it can bud no more; cut the stream from its fountain, the remnant will be dried up. Thus the Church, flooded with the light of the Lord, puts forth her rays through the whole world, yet with one light, which is spread upon all places, while its unity of Body is not infringed. She stretches forth her branches over the universal Earth, in the riches of plenty, and pours abroad her bountiful and onward streams; yet there is one Head, one Source, one Mother, abundant in the results of her fruitfulness." [By this Head, Source, and Mother St. Cyprian does not understand the Roman Church, nor the Roman Primate, but the *one undivided Episcopate*, which is only represented by the Primate. As soon as the Primate does not represent this Unity, he is judged by St. Cyprian's own words (chap. 5) : 'Qui pacem Christi et concordiam rumpit adversus Christum facit.... Et quisquam credit hanc unitatem de divina firmitate venientem, sacramentis cœlestibus cohærentem, *scindi in ecclesia posse et voluntatum collidentium divortio separari?* Hanc unitatem qui non tenet Dei legem non tenet, non tenet patris et filii fidem, vitam non tenet et salutem.' (Chap. 6) 'Hoc unitatis sacramentum, hoc vinculum *concordiæ inseparabiliter cohærentis* ostenditur, quando in evangelio tunica domini Jesu Christi *non dividitur omnino, nec scinditur,* sed sortientibus de veste Christi, quis Christum potius indueret, integra vestis accipitur et incorrupta atque *indivisa* tunica possidetur..... Unitatem illa portabat de superiore parte venientem, id est, *de cœlo et a patre venientem* (behold the source of unity !), quæ ab accipiente ac possidente *scindi omnino non poterat, sed totam simul et solidam firmitatem inseparabiliter obtinebat.* POSSIDERE NON POTEST INDUMENTUM CHRISTI QUI SCINDIT ET DIVIDIT ECCLESIAM CHRISTI.' [What an awful doom of Papacy from the mouth of this very Cyprian !]

We have only one remark to subjoin on the preceding passage of St. Cyprian, respecting St. Matt. xvi. 18. We find, according to Launoy's computation, that *forty-four* Fathers understand this passage as a declaration that Christ has founded His Church on the fundamental doctrine of His Divinity, which St. Peter so gloriously professed.

Seventeen Fathers only understood Christ's words to the effect, that He had founded the Church on St. Peter. (See Perrone: " Prælectiones Theologicæ." Paris, 1842, tom. II. p. 911 *seq.*) What is to be inferred from this scrutiny of Tradition? That there existed *no Apostolical Tradition* on the meaning of the said passage, and that every Father interpreted the words as he thought the meaning would best agree with the deposit of the Catholic faith. Had there existed an Apostolic tradition either way, the Churches would have known it, and no discordant interpretation could have originated. Could e. g. St. Augustine and St. Jerome really believe in the Pope's Supremacy, and still write as follows? St. Augustine (in Joan. Evang. tract. 124, 5): " Ecclesia non cadit, quoniam fundata est supra petram, unde Petrus nomen accepit, non enim a Petro petra, sed Petrus a petra, sicut non Christus a Christiano, sed Christianus a Christo vocatur . . . *Petra enim erat Christus*, super quod fundamentum etiam ipse ædificatus est Petrus (1 Cor. iii. 11)."—St. Jerome (in Amos vi. 12): " *Petra Christus est*, qui donavit apostolis suis, ut ipsi quoque petræ vocentur." Now if the Supremacy was, avowedly, so little known in the fourth and fifth centuries, what have we to think of Dr. Newman's Ante-Nicene testimonies? Or did they know, in the fourth century, less of the same than we do? Or were they less Catholic than the people of our days? *Or are the Roman Catholics of our days less Catholic than they?* There exists a Doctrinal Development in the Church, as we see clearly in the development of the doctrine on the Person of Christ, from Arianism to Monotheletism. But this development is made by œcumenical Councils on the ground of an existing Apostolical tradition. Such a tradition may be orally transmitted, so that, in the remaining written documents, little or nothing has been said of it. But this state of apparent dormancy cannot be applied to the Supremacy; for the discrepancy of opinions on this matter, uttered by the greatest doctors and luminaries of the Church, and *the overwhelming majority of the Fathers contradicting Supremacy*, show, beyond the slightest doubt, that they did not know of a respective tradition, and supposing they knew of a tradition, this tradition was rather the other way. Thus St. Cyprian speaks out his private judgment on the meaning of St. Matt. xvi. 18, and follows his master Tertullian, who with the skill of a clever solicitor looked, also in religious matters, for a *legal basis* of the *fait accompli*. When he—as St. Jerome relates (Catalog. cp. 53)—every day read the writings of Tertullian and said to his secretary: " Da Magistrum !" he was by and by imbued with Tertullian's legal mode of thinking. Moreover the African Church had a pronounced leaning towards the Roman, because they were so near to each other, entertained a frequent commerce, and spoke the same language. Still the African Church preserved its independence as a national Church. A. Ritschl (" Die Entstehung der altkatholischen Kirche," 2nd edit. p. 572 *seq.*) remarks very appositely: " Allerdings hat Cyprian das Bedürfniss, *die Einheit der Bischöfe* auf einen mehr empirischen Ausdruck zu bringen, und dasselbe hat ihn zur theoretischen Aufstellung der Voraussetzungen des römischen Primates [i. e. Supremates] geführt, obgleich er diese Gestalt der kirchlichen Einheit ebensowenig theoretisch gefolgert hat, als er sie praktisch anerkannte. Die Einheit der Bischöfe wird von ihm in der Person des Petrus angeschaut, welcher die auf die Bischöfe übergegangenen apostolischen Attribute zuerst empfangen hat. Um des Petrus willen wird sogar die römische Gemeinde, in welcher er der erste Bischof gewesen sein soll, als die Stammgemeinde der ganzen Kirche und als die Wurzel des bischöflichen Amtes geehrt. *Allein wie er die übrigen Apostel dem Petrus in Hinsicht ihrer Auktorität gleichstellt, so behauptet er keinen Vorzug des Nachfolgers des Petrus über die andern Bischöfe, sondern setzt sich dem Anspruch auf einen solchen entgegen."*

That our Saviour conferred the Primacy (within the limits above stated) on St. Peter is generally taught by the Fathers. I only mention, for instance's sake, St. Cyril of Alexandria in his Comment. on St. Luke (Oxford, 1859, p. 675): "To humble therefore our tendency to superciliousness, and *to repress ambitious feelings*, Christ shows that even he who seemed to be great is nothing and infirm. He therefore passes by the other disciples, and turns to him *who is the foremost, and set at the head of the company*." But this *personal* Primacy had nothing to do with the succeeding ecclesiastical Primacy. If St. Peter's successor was to be the next Primate, why was just the Bishop of

Rome this Primate? Had not Antioch the right of Primogeniture? Had Rome's Church been founded not by St. Peter but by some other apostle, it would have still held Primacy. Its paramount importance formed its right of Primogeniture, as Constantinople had, on the same principle, the Secundogeniture. That the Primate St. Peter founded the Church of the Roman Primate naturally suggested the idea of a *nexus causalis* between both, which idea, however, is not borne out by a consonant tradition.

We have done commenting on Dr. Newman's passage, and merely subjoin the phrase following it (Developm. p. 23): "Whatever objections may be made to this or that particular fact, and *I do not think any valid ones can be raised* [?!], still, on the whole, I consider that a cumulative argument rises from them in favour of the active and the doctrinal authority of Rome." Mr. Allies ("The Engl. Ch. cleared," p. 62) justly remarks: "Mr. Newman suggests that 'all authority necessarily leads to resistance'" (Develop. p. 24). In that point of view, certainly, the first four centuries supply the strongest sort of 'cumulative argument' to the Roman Supremacy, *for they are nothing else but a perpetual denial of it.*" The result of our researches is, that we found the Popes Victor and Stephen attempting, most unsuccessfully, to introduce Supremacy, but that they could not stand the force of ancient tradition against their innovation. The passages of ancient Fathers adduced in support of Supremacy are *all misinterpreted*, and their argument, therefore, crumbles into dust. This our result is distinctly corroborated by the greatest Fathers of the fourth and fifth centuries, who in explaining St. Matt. xvi. 18 did not know anything of Supremacy, consequently they could not have understood the alleged passages as Dr. Newman understood them. Where is now Dr. Newman's *germ to be developed?* Had, during three centuries, not a single word been said about Supremacy, the matter would have been rather doubtful, but a mere theorist might have pleaded the *dormancy* of the respective tradition. Now, on the contrary, the matter at issue was brought forward, but *piteously fell to the ground on account of its novelty*. Thus Papal Supremacy took its rise from *Ambition*,

> the fruit
> Of that forbidden tree, whose mortal taste
> Brought death into the world, and all our woe,

which vice is rooted the deepest in the heart of man. When the Pope first attempted to take steps in this direction, *Victor* was easily made a *Victus*, as he had no traditional ground to stand upon. But Stephen had already a precedent in Victor; and with every ambitious Pope the number of precedents grew, and the number of arguments too; for ambition and imperiousness are most ingenious in finding out plausible reasons and evidences in favour of their proceedings, and thus "*veritatem subtilitate frustrantur*" (St. Cyprian). "And thus we see opinions, usages, and systems, *which are of venerable and imposing aspect, but which have no soundness within them, and keep together from a habit of consistence*" (Dr. Newman: On Development, p. 92). Papacy went on briskly, conquered both the ecclesiastical and the secular world, pleaded the *jus præscriptionis*, and built up a system of papal rights, in spite of powerful Councils (Constance and Basle) contesting the same. Papacy was, by these ominous signs of the times, not stopped in its onward course, till it burst like a ripe ulcer, and Reformation carried off half the Roman Catholic Church. Rome was cut off from the Orthodox Church, and *the Orthodox Church remained undivided up to the present hour*, whereas the Roman Church, doomed by schism, was decomposed by a new schism. On which side is here soundness of the body?—Then a new religious order arose to elevate Papacy from its utter humiliation. The order called itself *the Society of Jesus* (sicut lucus a non lucendo), and represented *the very essence of Papacy*. Its aim is to support Papacy at any price, to instil the papal doctrines into the mind of the people, and thus to create by and by a new traditional basis, to which ancient tradition must either yield or be adapted. These are the *tactics* of the Jesuits which I have more fully disclosed in my German book: "Die orthodoxe katholische Anschauung" (the first 33 pages). I here insert one passage (p. 7 *seq.*) to show what the working and influence of Jesuitism was since its re-admission into Germany in 1848, and how they assisted or rather guided the Pope in bringing out the last dogma of the Immaculate Conception of the blessed Virgin Mary.

"Soon the Jesuits found out how to attach to themselves the reinvigorated life of Catholicism, to make out themselves and Catholicism to be one and the same thing; or rather, to assume to be its crowning glory. They introduced their writings and doctrinal manuals, promulgated the Ultramontane *placita* of their Order, and sought to rivet the attention of Christians on what is exclusively Romish and external; and they succeeded in carrying their point, and accordingly, in themselves determining what development the Church should take. This part of the subject requires further explanation, and is well worth studying. The Jesuit order, in addition to the three ordinary vows, takes a fourth—that of unconditional and unlimited obedience to the Pope. This promise is a serious thing, but is very easy to make ; for if the Pope conforms strictly to the will of the Jesuits, these may very well be conformable to the Pope, i. e. only to themselves. It is, therefore, nothing but a vow of *egoism*, in which one vows to have one's own way. Should it please the Pope to will anything displeasing to the Jesuits, their obedience would be as edifying as at the time of Clement XIV., when the pious fathers themselves set at nought his fulminations, and under the ægis of heretical and schismatical princes, persisted in maintaining an institute Rome no longer acknowledged. So far did they go in their pride, that they regarded themselves as indispensable, and in all seriousness claimed to be more Catholic than the Pope. This is what suggests to the witty Romans the saying, *Il papa nero vale più del papa bianco*. 'The black Pope (the General of the Jesuits, who wears black) is of more consequence than the white Pope (since the Pope always wears a white *soutane*).' Since, according to this proverb, the Jesuit Order is above the Pope, and knows how to rule the Pope so cleverly, that he fancies he himself is sovereign, the main and vital question with the order must be this—how to manage so as to secure for the Pope, i. e. for themselves, the sole and definite power in all that concerns the doctrine and life of the Church, or in other words, *unlimited dominion*.—What is to be done, therefore, is to make the hitherto undecided scholastic opinion of *the Infallibility of the Pope* an article of faith (*dogma explicitum*). But how to attain this object ? Hitherto, the way in which *dogmata implicita*, i. e. opinions of the schools, in favour of which the majority of the Catholic world has declared, have been elevated to the rank of *dogmata explicita*, i. e. doctrinal articles received and published by the Church, has been by means of an œcumenical Council. Even in cases in which, owing to the times, such a Council has been an impossibility, and yet an opinion has fought its way to a certain degree of dogmatical authority, the next Council has nevertheless held it necessary to give a dogmatic sanction to such an article by means of a formal decree. The doctrine of Papal Infallibility has already been long ventilated in the schools, which is the less matter for surprise since it is the most repulsive indeed, but the inevitable, final deduction of the Papal system.—As now many an error at the outset springs from a germ very like a truth, and develops itself harmlessly for a good while, but at last cannot help revealing the inevitable and glaring false conclusion wrapt up within it, so was it with this last deduction. Many allowed themselves to dally with the Papacy in a milder and more limited form, who opened their eyes when they heard on all sides its last word sounding in their ears, and already imagined themselves the victims of its thundering *Quos ego !*— There is no overlooking the fact, that the Jesuits are the champions in this cause; but they remarked, also, that the most respectable men, and the greatest geniuses of their Church, i. e. all who retained any measure of independence, held aloof.* They were well aware, there-

---

* Against Papal Infallibility are [Kenrick (Theologia dogmatica)], Gengler, Möhler, Klee, Drey, Staudenmaier, Kuhn, Hefele, Dieringer, Pichler, i. e. all the leading men of German Roman-Catholicism. Döllinger, though leaning towards Papal Infallibility, censured (with Hefele) the proceedings of Pope Honorius, and had therefore to swallow the bitter effusions of the *Civiltà cattolica*, a Jesuit periodical highly approved by the Pope. Möhler's *Einheit der Kirche* did not please in Rome, but, up to his death, he never recanted. Pichler's work was censured, and—he recanted! Still Pichler based his statements on facts, and how can facts be retracted? Perrone, his pupil Dr. Reinerding, and Riess are, at this moment, the hottest defenders of Papal Infallibility, but I should like to know how they can remove the *seven difficulties* which Professor Dieringer in his review ("Theologisches Literaturblatt," Bonn, 1866, No. 5) has raised. For further information see Dieringer's " Lehrbuch der katholischen Dogmatik," 5th edit. 1865, p.

fore, that it was necessary to wait a while, and prudently to temporize; but as the wily general employs the time of seeming truce in pioneering and reconnoitring, so were they active otherwise than in direct attack. Their plan and course of reasoning, which they do not speak out, but only indicate by their course of procedure, is the following: —' Hitherto, articles of faith have only been made by the decrees of œcumenical Councils. This way is tedious, unpractical, and in the

---

624 *seq.*—Very different are the views of Archbishop Manning, Martin, and Ward. In fact, the views of the Gallicans, of Cardinal Cusa, de Veron, de Marca, Launoy, Antonio Pereira de Figueredo, Möhler, Pichler, &c., are much nearer the Orthodox notion of Primacy than the Ultramontane tenet of Papal Infallibility. And Dr. Neale and E. H. Landon draw still nearer the Orthodox Primacy. How different are the views of Dr. H. E. Manning, Archbishop of Westminster! In his pamphlet "The Reunion of Christendom" (London, 1866) he says, p. 65 *seq.*: " But if it be ill-advised to assail the mind of the Church, *it is still more so to oppose its visible Head.* There can be no doubt that the Sovereign Pontiff .... defined the Immaculate Conception, and that *he believes in his own infallibility.* If these things be our reproach, we share it with the Vicar of Jesus Christ. They are not our private opinions, nor the tenets of a school, but the mind of the Pontiff, as they were of his predecessors, as they will be of those who come after him. To appeal from the Pope to an ' Eighth ' General Council of Greeks, Anglicans, and Romans, who shall put down Ultramontanism, restore the Immaculate Conception to the region of pious opinions without foundation in Scripture and antiquity, *declare the Pope to be fallible,* and subject to General Councils ... reunite Christendom on the basis of the Russian Catechism ..... —all this is to us no harbinger of unity, no voice of peace, because no sign of humility, no evidence of faith." And again, p. 68: "... you will keep steadfastly to one point, namely, the perpetual infallibility of the Church, whether diffused, or in Council, whether speaking by the Council of Trent *or by its Head.* It is necessary to be on your guard against two modes of argument by which this affirmation is evaded. The one is to lead away into details ..... The other is to admit the perpetual Divine office of the Church, *denying the infallibility of its Head,* and of the Councils held since the schism of the Greek Church."

present case, unfavourable to our object. The unconditional obedience hitherto accorded to the Pope in disciplinary matters must be extended to the sphere of belief: the line between the two is not so definitely drawn as men think, for discipline and doctrine often border very closely on one another, and the examples in which the doctrinal tendencies of certain theologians, e. g. the systems of Hermes, Günther, Bautain, &c., have been prohibited, and the prohibition willingly accepted and acquiesced in, are as essentially precedents as the notification and condemnation of heretical books. But for all that, it is hazardous to make a general rule out of precedents ; and in our case it is doubly hazardous, since the judge would decide in his own cause. It would too greatly shock delicate feelings if the judge were to say, ' I, the judge, pronounce that I, the judge, am in the right.' Our numerous adversaries would be the more encouraged to rise against us, inasmuch as they could with truth affirm, that for more than eighteen centuries it has been a thing unheard of, that matters of faith can be settled otherwise than by a General Council. But if we venture upon our *coup* and lose, we lose for ever ; and, worse than all, down goes the belief in our omnipotence, and we no longer stand forth as the Unique Society, surrounded with a magic glory and a magic power. To be sure, it is not likely that we should exactly lose the day, but it is not a matter of indifference to us whether we win with a majority, however strong, or secure unanimity. Accordingly, we must still, for the present, content ourselves with biding our time, and making preparation. How to do this is clear. We must pave the way, i. e. we must level the road towards the method of deciding doctrines by the Pope alone, without a Council.' This was what they were driving at when, in their theological lectures and writings—especially in the hand-books of canon law—they gave to the Papal system the most decisive victory over the Episcopal.

" In the southern countries of Europe the way was already open ; and in the northern so great was the admiration of the newly-introduced Jesuits, that the soil was extremely favourable for the work. In France alone, the independent Gallican spirit was still the most formidable obstacle, but Rome had nevertheless so carried on her operations here—especially since the February revolution—that Ultramontanism had got the upper hand, particularly in the episcopate. Thus the ground was nearly everywhere prepared ; for Britain and the non-

European countries either procure their clergy from Rome, or at any rate, stand in the most intimate filial relation with her. But for the wary Jesuits, the anxiously expected moment of promulgating their dogma, and thereby attaining the summit of their glory, was not yet come. It was necessary first to make an essay with another article, and thus to see whether the path was clear—whether the bridge would bear.

"For this purpose, the elevation of the Immaculate Conception of the Virgin Mary—till then only a scholastic opinion—into a dogma, was made to serve the turn. The Protestants have entirely misunderstood the reason and the significance of this fact. Much has been written and spoken about the infringement of Christ's dignity as our only Redeemer, by means of this exaltation of the blessed Virgin, about the freedom of Mary's ancestors from original sin necessarily following from it, &c.; but all this is partly an incorrect view of the dogma, and partly exaggeration. *The true centre of gravity of this event lies, not in the present, but in the future,* in so far as this new method of deciding on doctrines, which has actually been tried with success, affords a sure guarantee that the next dogma to be set up, that of the Infallibility of the Pope, will be proclaimed without difficulty. Hence the general fermentation now prevalent. The Catholics allowed the doctrine to be proclaimed, and held their peace, because they deemed this article of faith of no great moment; and now they discover that they have allowed their hands to be tied, and that they will justly be chargeable with inconsistency when they shall want to reject the same course of procedure in the case of the next dogma. . . . . The first and highest desire of Pope Pius is towards his heavenly mother, Mary. Accordingly, the Jesuits managed with great tact and circumspection when they attacked the Pope on this side, and, besides, they could reckon on a wide circle of sympathizers. They acted with foresight on this ground also, since they exalted the *external* veneration of the blessed Virgin at the expense of the *internal* honouring and invocation of the Virgin, which latter rests on Mary's justification and sanctification through the redeeming merits of Christ, and they were thus enabled to help on still further the externalizing of Christianity.

"*Externalism is superficiality; superficiality is frivolity; frivolity means manageableness by a strong spirit and will:* thus is the riddle solved. Saint Mary cannot be more honoured than she was before the publication of the dogma. An increase of pomp and glory at her festivals attracts the masses, but repels the more reflective. Where the eye has too much to see, where the fumes of incense and the odours of sweet-smelling flowers bewitch one, and the whole outward man and his senses have too much to do, no room is left for the spirit and the heart. The man thus externalized is easily governed. Lastly, the Jesuits acted prudently in their selection of the point to be raised to the dignity of a dogma, since they base their polemics upon the cultus of St. Mary. '*Maria, tu sola interemisti hæreses in universo mundo!*'—so runs the antiphony for the Festival of the Conception of the Blessed Virgin Mary. Thus their zeal was in a certain sense a question in which the honour of their patroness was concerned. But all these motives which led them to pitch on this dogma are, nevertheless, of so little comparative consequence, that they are thrust into the shade by the one true motive, viz. the desire to make the experiment, in the case of another and an unsuspected doctrine, whether the new method of deciding doctrinal questions would meet with insurmountable obstacles, and whether the same path might not be struck into to reach the fundamental dogma to be hereafter laid down, that of Papal Infallibility.

"Moreover, it is worth while to look at the antecedents of this new dogmatical phenomenon. The sentence was not sent forth so very abruptly. Years before the bishops of the Catholic world were besought by the Pope to consult the theological faculties of their respective Universities, and to report upon the popular belief within their dioceses. Meanwhile the Pope did not hide the fact that he himself was entirely persuaded of the truth of the dogma about to be proclaimed. This last circumstance was alone sufficient to determine the opinion of most of the bishops. The Pope's anxiety to know the popular belief of the various dioceses, and, accordingly, his laying stress on the quality of the popular belief, cannot but excite surprise, since, according to the theory hitherto received, only the Episcopate has the right to testify as to the purity of Catholic doctrine, and the lay world is not consulted at all. The meaning of that inquiry can, therefore, only have been this,—it was wanted to know whether the novelty would be likely to scandalize the people, and to produce schisms, or whether, on the other hand, the seed scattered to this end in former days had already borne its fruits, and had familiarized men with the thing. This was certainly the case, since the devotional manuals of the Jesuits Wille, Nakatenus, Devis, &c., were the most widely circulated amongst the people. (*That is the way how Roman traditions are fabricated and instilled into the minds of the people !*) When in this way the opinions of the bishops had arrived at Rome, and an apparent *consensus* of the *ecclesia dispersa* had been attained, it was already possible to take further steps.

"It was argued, that since the judgment of the Church had been obtained, it was just as valid as if the bishops who voted had been assembled in Council; but it is just this which is false, for according to Catholic belief, it is not in the isolated bishop, but in the episcopate, as a whole, that the prerogative of infallibility inheres. Now every one must see that a body with free discussion and minute investigation of every doubt and scruple, cannot but lead to quite other results than a one-sided query, with a pretty clear hint as to the answer desired. If the divine-human energy (das theandrische Moment) —that is, the co-operation of God's Spirit and human freedom—ought visibly to pervade the entire activity of the Church, in this case human freedom was restrained to a very essential extent. Instead of summoning a Council, the Jesuit maxim, *Divide et impera*, was followed. When now the dogmatic decision was so far ready that nothing but its publication was waited for, the Pope called together a considerable number of bishops to Rome,—more, indeed, than had been assembled at many an important Council; but he declared expressly that he had not summoned them for the purpose of giving a decision, but only to join in the celebration of the ceremonial of publication.

"Accordingly, it is worthy of remark, as a stroke of policy, that the Pope was not allowed to proceed so summarily, but that certain formalities, consultations, congregations, were added, in order thereby to conceal the unusual character of the new method. But for all that the Pope protests expressly that he is assembling no Council around him for the purpose, and in this protest we have the entire new method foreshadowed, that is, the Pope's all-sufficiency for the creation of new dogmas. The previous consultation of the bishops by the Pope is a free act of his own, not enjoined by any law of the Church, and depends entirely upon his arbitrary will.

"Indeed, if we now go a step farther, we see that in the dogma of the Immaculate Conception, that of the Infallibility of the Pope *is already pronounced*, nay, more, *is already practically applied*, *already anticipated ! ! !*

" According to the foregoing, the Pope, in his plenitude of power, has finally determined and declared the dogma respecting Mary. The Roman Catholic Church has accepted it, and accordingly has solemnly acknowledged the Pope's right to declare it, has set her seal to the divine truth of his *dictum*, i. e. *has proclaimed his Infallibility*. Accordingly, it can be nothing more than a mere formality, a simple piece of child's play, if it be desired to promulgate the Papal Infallibility as a dogma in strict form. The article has only to be proposed with the stroke of a pen, and the unanimous assent of all must be assured; for the gainsayer will only need to be asked, 'Why do you believe in the Immaculate Conception of Mary?' Answer, 'Because the Pope has said it.' *Ergo*, he is Infallible. The doctrine of a tacit consent of the Church, which some would gladly interpolate as a saving clause, is a convenient device, but is plainly at variance with the fact, that opinions which have passed current as those of the Church have never become formal, and consequently binding dogmas, until they have been expressly sanctioned by the next general Council.

[" Pichler ('Geschichte der kirchlichen Trennung, &c.' tom. I. p. 496) reports an interesting incident which I did not know eight years ago—when the above pages were first printed—since Pitzipios divulged the fact only in 1860. Pichler says: 'Respecting the Papal claims to personal Infallibility, Pitzipios appealed already in 1860, and again in his reply to the Pope himself (1862), to an incident of which we heard nothing from other sides. Pitzipios says, 'The position which we held at the time when the Council at Rome, in the year 1854, was assembled, did not allow us to remain ignorant that in this meeting, which consisted almost exclusively of Romanists,—un cardinal se leva *au nom du saint siége et proposa*, puisqu'on se trouvait ainsi réunis, de définir en même temps sans plus de façons le dogme de l'infallibilité du pape. Un morne silence accueillit d'abord cette brusque proposition. Puis s'élevèrent des murmures. C'est une surprise! C'est un piége! se disaient entre eux les prelats.' Two bishops stood up protesting against the proposition, and thus the question was put aside.'— I suppose the exclamations *surprise*, *piége !* must not have been very serious, since in the *very numerous Council only two Bishops* took heart to protest. Rome desisted from proclaiming this new dogma, for two novelties at once would have been too much. Rome wanted, for the moment, only a *feeler* but no decree of a Council. And this feeler was favourable beyond expectation. Had not even the Immaculate Conception more opposers?]

"This is the serious aspect of the time; this causes the secret fermentation which we find going on in the Roman Catholic Church, when we look at its doctrinal tendencies. The Jesuitical impulses at work in this matter are plain; the Jesuitical interests and those of the Romish Church here coalesce. An ecclesiastical schism on a grand scale was generally looked for, when the new dogma was published, just as when Günther's system was condemned a wide-spread revolt of this powerful school was expected. Neither event happened. And it is well that it did not happen. For what would have come out of it? A separate camp of semi-Catholics, which would soon have collapsed, like Jansenism, for example. But a secret fermentation, a widespread dissatisfaction of the most gifted spirits within the Roman-Catholic Church, is the characteristic of our age. The ferment is still a secret one, for men may rather be said to be sensible of the oppressiveness and uncomfortableness of their ecclesiastical condition than to have a clear insight into the Catholic belief and life. It would be a great misfortune if this process of fermentation were to be interrupted by any premature general secession; it must follow its natural course, and lead to the conviction that in Christianity there are only two ways possible, that of the autocratic Papacy, and that of Orthodox-Catholic freedom,—a middle course is impossible. When men are discontented with the Church of the fully developed Papacy, nothing but a transition to the truly Evangelical freedom of the Orthodox Catholic Church is possible."

All the opponents of Romanism bring forward *the practical working* of its system as a test of its want of Catholicity. However, most of the Protestant antagonists are so remarkably unhandy in wielding this weapon that the Romans easily overthrow them. Still the Romans feel uneasy in their combat, betraying a certain misgiving as to the end of this struggle. Dr. Pusey attacked the practical system of the Romish devotion to the B. V. M., and Dr. Newman repulsed him by disowning Dr. Faber's and other individual effusions; but the popular devotion prevalent in all Southern Roman Catholic countries, countenanced by the modern Saint Alfonso de Liguori, is not so easily shaken off. Here we want an explanation and justification. Dr. Newman does not sympathize with that Southern devotion, and prefers the English mode. In his "Letter to Dr. Pusey on his Eirenicon" (p. 22) he says: "I prefer English habits of *belief and devotion* to foreign, from the same causes, and by the same right, which justifies foreigners in preferring their own. In following those of my people, I show less singularity, and create less disturbance than if I made a flourish with what is novel and exotic." [But the *Solidarity* of the several parts of the Church effects that, depravation obtaining in any part of the Church, the consequences affect the whole, and the guilt is to be borne by the whole.] Then he points to "Dr. Griffith, the late Vicar-Apostolic of the London district. He warned me against books of devotion of the Italian school, which were just at that time coming into England .... I did not understand that he was jealous of all Italian books, ... but I took him to *caution me against a character and tone of religion*, excellent in its place, not suited for England .... If at that time [after Dr. Newman's return to England] I was betrayed into any acts which were of a more extreme character than I should approve now, the responsibility of course is mine; but the impulse came, not from old Catholics or superiors, but from men whom I loved and trusted, who were younger than myself. But to whatever extent I might be carried away, . . . my mind in no long time fell back to what seems to me a *safer* and more practical course." But local or national influences which affect a dogma or its practical bearing to such an extent that Dr. Griffith had to caution Dr. Newman against books of that class, seem not to be so innocuous as the Romans might make us believe. I lived a couple of years in Rome, and had plenty of opportunity to witness this extreme devotion to the B. V. It would not be derogatory to the Church-belief, indeed, if it was only practised by individuals, opposed by individuals, discussed by individuals. But as soon as it grows into a national practice, it settles down and crystallizes erroneous views and usages so as to become the basis of new abuses. In fact Dr. Newman touches only upon this subject, but does not even try to defend it. This is exactly the way how Roman Primacy grew into Supremacy, how out of the *Redemptiones* in the " Libri Pœnitentiales " were made *Indulgences*, how the belief in the Immaculate Conception was first made popular and then a dogma. But how may a Romish Saint countenance a practice which you do not approve of ? A Saint who, in the process of canonization, stood his ground against the " Advocatus Diaboli " ? A Saint, whose books are approved by the Pope, and whose views

Pope Gregory XVI. expressly allowed to be held by every Roman Catholic? Dr. Newman answers (p. 103): "The greatest name is St. Alphonso Liguori; but it never surprises me to read anything unusual in the devotions of a saint. Such men are on a level very different from our own, and *we cannot understand them*. [Thus only can the Gordian knot be cut!] I hold this to be an important canon in the Lives of the Saints .... But we may refrain from judging, without proceeding to imitate." No doubt, there is some truth at the bottom of the canon which Dr. Newman lays down for judging the lives of the saints. However, I hold this to be another and more important canon: "But though we, or an angel from heaven, preach any other gospel unto you than that which we have preached unto you, let him be accursed" (Galat. i. 8).

We saw that Dr. Newman's defence of Roman practices is rather reserved. But how different is the language of Archbishop Manning. There is no tergiversation, but plain outspoken Romish teaching. If Dr. Newman is about to say, Let me alone! What are the Italian practices to me, an Englishman? Archbishop Manning says ("The Reunion of Christendom," p. 65): " If *sentire cum Ecclesia* be a test of conformity to the mind of the Spirit, *Ecclesiæ dissentire* is no sign of illumination; for the presence and assistance of the Holy Ghost which secures the Church within the sphere of faith and morals, *invests it also with instincts and a discernment which preside over its worship and doctrine, its practices and customs. We may be sure that whatsoever is preva-*

lent in the Church, under the eye of its public authority, practised by the people, and not censured by its pastors, is at least conformable to faith, and innocent as to morals. Whosoever rises up to condemn such practices and opinions, thereby convicts himself of the private spirit, which is the root of heresy." Thus Archbishop Manning finds the practice of the *Bambino* at Rome not objectionable? The less said of it the better, but suffice it to say that good Roman Catholics find it *absurd* and *scandalous*. And what will the Archbishop say to the following Inscription which I myself copied from the walls of the Church of SS. Pudens and Pudentiana in Rome in the year 1852? I give it exactly as it stands, in its old orthography with its grammatical faults, line by line, Latin and Italian (which, in that Church, face each other on the opposite walls). Here you have a document placed " under the eye of the public authority of the Church " in the very head-quarters of Romanism.

In hac omnium ecclesiarum urbis vetustissima olim domo S. Pudentis
Senatoris, patris SS. Novatii et Timothei, et SS. Pudentianæ et Praxedis
    Virg.
Fuit SS. Apostolorum Petri et Pauli hospitium primum, ad martyrum,
Et Christianorum baptismum, et ad missas sacramque sinaxim . sub
    altare
Jacent tria millia corpora SS. Martyrum, et copiosus Sanctorum sanguis ;
Visitantes hanc eccliam singulis diebus consequuntur indulgentiam
    trium
-Millium annorum et remissionem tertie partis peccatorum suorum,
    aliasque
Quam plurimas, et præsertim in die stationis quæ est feria tertia
Post tertiam dominicam quadragesimæ et in festis SS. Pudentis et
        Pudentianæ.

The Italian translation on the south-wall.

In questa chiesa più antiqua delle altre di Roma già casa di San Pudente
Senatore padre de SS. Novatio Timotheo et delle SS. Vergini Pudentiana et
Prassede ; fù il primo alogiamento delli SS. Apostoli Pietro et Paulo, et dove
Si batezzavano coloro che si facevano Christiani, et si radunavano per udire
le messe, et ricevere la Santa Comunione.
Vi sono sepulti I corpi di tre milla Martiri et racolto copioso sangue di Martiri
Coloro che visitano questa chiesa ogni giorno conseguiscono indulgenza di
Tre milla anni, et la remissione della terza parte di loro peccati, et molte
Altre, e principalmente nel giorno della statione qual' è nella terza feria
Doppo la terza domenica di quaresima, et nelle feste di SS. Pudente et Pudentiana.

I will not speak of the impossibility that *three thousand* bodies of martyrs should rest under the altar, as the Italian translator himself seems to have felt this difficulty, and generally translates, " There are buried three thousand," &c. Of course, if the Church of S. Ursula at Cologne comprises the bodies of *Ten thousand* Virgin Martyrs, why should not that of SS. Pudente e Pudenziana have three thousand martyrs?—But now to proceed to the *Indulgence of three thousand years daily to be gained* by those who visit the said Church, Pope Benedict XIV. (" De Synodo diœcesana," lib. XIII., cap. 18, no. 9), and the decree of the 18th Sept., 1669, declare all Indulgences of thousand years and upwards *not to be genuine.* And according to Thom. Aquinas there must be a ratio between the indulgence and the works required. This is the consonant teaching of Bouvier, Giraud, P. A. Maurel, S.J., Dr. V. Gröne ("Der Ablass, seine Geschichte und Bedeutung in der Heilsökonomie," 1863), &c. But theory and practice are, in the Roman system, two very different things, as you may observe, moreover, in the "*altaria privilegiata*" which you meet with in most of the churches in Rome. They are against the letter of the law (cf. Gröne, p. 149, no. 5; p. 151, no. 15), but in daily use. Nevertheless, the Archbishop has "no hesitation in saying, that whosoever shall rise up to condemn as pernicious what the public authority of the Church tolerates as innocent, is thereby guilty of temerity, and of immodesty. In so doing he would be ascribing to himself the supreme discernment which belongs to the Church alone. . . . It would be the illuminism of the individual revising the discernment of the Church; the climax and efflorescence of the private judgment which criticizes all things—first Scripture, then Fathers, then Churches, then Councils, then Pontiffs, finally the accumulated living Christianity of the Catholic Church, in which the heart and mind of Fathers, Councils, and Pontiffs breathe, and teach, and worship" (p. 38). Here you have that *lifeless mechanical Churchdom* where the Individual reckons for nothing, and is simply swallowed up *in gurgite vasto.* Of course, such notions do not allow the Churchman "to be led away into *details.*" "This has the effect of diversion, and the main issue is left without an answer" (p. 68). This is far from true; for every whole consists of the assemblage of its component parts, and refusing to deal with details you cannot reach the system which grows up out of details. If the details are untenable, its result cannot be tenable.—Such notions show the tyranny of the Roman Church-authority, by which the individual is, *spiritually*, crushed to atoms before forming a sound part of the Church. But this tyranny does not stop here; it affects *the body* also! Pope Pius IX. in his last Encyclical says: " Namque ipsos minime pudet affirmare..... Ecclesiæ jus non competere violatores legum suarum *pœnis temporalibus coercendi.*" And in the Syllabus (No. 24) he brands as an error the proposition: "Ecclesia *vis inferendæ potestatem* non habet, neque potestatem ullam temporalem directam vel indirectam." This strongly smells of the sweet fumes of *stakes*, certainly much to the delight of Englishmen, *the freest people of the world*, who are not particularly fond of flogging, torturing, and burning. Is there any Englishman who can forget Cowper's admirable verses?

> Slaves cannot breathe in England ‡ if their lungs
> Receive our air, that moment they are free ;
> They touch our country, and their shackles fall.

Thus the Pope claims, in matter of religion, "the power of using force and inflicting temporal punishment!" On the contrary, the Koran (Surah II. 257) says: "Lâ ikrâha fi'ddîn." ("There is no constraint with regard to religion.") And Maximus, Patriarch of Constantinople, in his missive to the Doge Giovanni Mocenigo of Venice (A. D. 1480) : " Νόμον θεοῦ εἶναι τὸ ἀβίαστον " ("that unconstraint was the law of God"). How much to the point does the heathen Tacitus exclaim (Agricola, cp. 32) : " Metus et terror est, *infirma vincla caritatis;* quæ ubi removeris, qui timere desierint, *odisse* incipient." This thought is masterly developed by Thucydides (III. 43—49).

—That the actual power of the Pope is too weak and insignificant to carry out what he claims, is of less consequence than the fact that he really claims it, and, occasionally may carry out what he now only claims. Cyriaque Lampryllos (" Le Turban et la Tiare," Paris, 1865, p. 11) remarks to the point : " Il y a un mahométisme fort et un mahométisme faible, comme il arrive aussi du *papisme* ou de toute autre croyance *qui professe le droit de la contrainte en matière de la religion,*—atroces et arrogants quand ils disposent de la force matérielle, accomodants et patelins lorsqu'elle leur échappe.—*L'église orientale,*—et que cela soit dit à son éternel honneur,—*n'a jamais professé ce principe* ANTI-CHRÉTIEN. *Elle l'a toujours repoussé, par la voix de ses hiérarques et de ses docteurs, dans tous les cas et en toute occasion. Elle l'a solennellement* CONDAMNÉ *lors du concile tenu à Sainte-Sophie pour la réprobation des accommodements de Florence.*" And what does such a government make of its subjects? No wonder that Pope Innocent III, (in his letter to Boniface of Montferrat, in the year 1205) speaks of the Greek Church, "quæ in Latinis non nisi perditionis exempla et opera tenebrarum aspexit, ut jam MERITO *illos abhorreat plus quam canes* " (De Bréquigny, Epist. Innoc. III. lib. VIII. ep. 133, tom. II. p. 769).

Now I repeat my words (p. 114) :

Where is the Catholic Church? This is naturally the first question of all serious Anglican Reunionists. Is it the Eastern or the Western Church? Both do not agree; both disclaim one another's title to sound catholicity. Both cannot go together. Therefore the wise Reunionist knows he must *choose.*

The choice would be comparatively easy if in this case the head alone had to decide, but *"men go by their sympathies, not by argument;* and if I feel the force of this influence myself, who bow to the arguments, why may not others still more who never have in the same degree admitted the arguments?" These words of Dr. Newman ("Apologia pro vita sua," p. 237) remind me of Lord Chesterfield's advice: "When they come to be a little better acquainted with themselves, and with their own species, they discover that *plain right reason is, nine times in ten, the fettered and shackled attendant of the triumph of the heart and the passions;* consequently they address themselves nine times in ten to the conqueror, not to the conquered." This is the clue to THE MYSTERY OF ROME'S ATTRACTIVENESS. The question naturally arises, why have almost all seceders from the English Church gone over to Rome? And many a one of these, hostile to Rome and addicted to Orthodoxy, veered round in the last moment, and seemed to say: "*Invitus trahor!*" Still this mystery is not so mysterious as one would think, and there are plenty of reasons how to account for such an apparently strange phenomenon. Part of these reasons I adduced above, p. 115 *seq.* Part I will hint at now.

1. Most of the seceders had wandered for a long time in search of the true Catholic Church. Tired by their labours, they longed for *rest.* Inviting voices, outstretched hands, supporting arms of their Roman friends and countrymen led them to their Church, and the last obstacles were removed by a hearty welcome from enthusiastic lips.—2. Rest they wanted, rest they found, and a deeper rest than Orthodoxy ever could offer them; for *they acquiesce in the visible Pope's divine oracles,* whereas Orthodoxy has only *the invisible Holy Ghost's working in the Church.* Poor Orthodoxy has only *seven* œcumenical councils—rich Romanism has *seventeen* (or *nineteen*) general councils, and many dogmatical decisions besides, and is fast developing its doctrinal system under the Pope's guidance. How pleasant to have such ready help

in all difficulties! How satisfactory for human inquisitiveness to have later and fuller information from heavenly regions! How attractive for students and divines to have a more extensive basis of operation, a more detailed system of theology! How secure to travel on the high-road garnished by innumerable hand-posts warning not to trespass on the inviolable fields of dogmatical decisions! "ALL DEPENDS ON THE FACT OF THE SUPREMACY OF ROME" (Dr. Newman: "On Anglican Difficulties," 2nd edit. p. 284). And if this Supremacy proves to be a failure—your rest is gone! Or will you slumber on, distracted by doubt and fear, on the brink of a precipice?—3. The Romans are more numerous than the Orthodox. The charm of the Majority was already felt by St. Jerome, when he wondered that almost the whole Christian world had become *Arian* (as it since has become *Papal*). When the ten tribes forsook their Lord, the Minority of the two remained faithful to Him (see above, p. 94).—4. The *Headship of the Pope*, once lawful and recognized by the whole Church, but forfeited by schism and since devolved on the Patriarch of Constantinople, continues exercising a strong influence on the minds.—5. *Exempla trahunt* is a true saying. There was made a start from Anglicanism to Romanism, and its influence is going on still. Those who went before attracted, by an open or hidden process, those who were left behind. And this attracting power shows itself to be mightier with those who once protested most bitterly than with those who seemed the nearest. Psychology solves this enigma; for " les extrémités se touchent."

THE NEXT STEP.

IF your choice decides against Rome and in favour of Orthodoxy, what must be your *next step*?

Is it your duty, or is it even advisable, to join the *Eastern* Church? You are *Westerns*, and you never can put off your Western mode of thinking and living (see above, p. 59 *seq.* and p. 21). But the Orthodox Church neither requires nor wishes you to adopt the Eastern form. Whether Eastern or Western is all the same to her, she only insists upon Orthodoxy. However, the *actually existing* Western Church has separated itself from the Orthodox East, so that, presently, there is no Orthodox Western Church. But if there exists no Orthodox Western Church, *there ought to exist one*. Indeed the Papal West tried, at different times, to entice the East, and to replace Orthodoxy by Papacy, thus repairing the schism by a *Unity of Error*. Political straits and complications in the East were taken advantage of to induce some Eastern Bishops to take part in Western Councils, but their proceedings were disapproved of by their brother Bishops, and condemned by the Orthodox people at large. The sham-Union was at once rescinded. In fact, Rome has shown most clearly that it will not submit to Orthodoxy, but that it will subdue Orthodoxy. This statement fully justifies OUR TASK TO BUILD UP AGAIN THE ORTHODOX WESTERN CHURCH, stone by stone, individual by individual, congregation by congregation, since the bulk of the Western Church continues resisting Orthodoxy. As we cannot begin from *above*, uniting the two wholes, we must begin from *below*, gathering single members, and thus, in a long process, recruit the 'Orthodox Western Church. This task requires time and patience, labour and perseverance, circumspection and energy, courage and confidence. Out of a grain of mustard seed Christendom sprang up, covering the wide world, for our Saviour had sown it. We must again sow this least of all seeds, and our Saviour will mature it. We must begin at once to " build again the tabernacle which is fallen down, and to build again the ruins thereof, and to set it up ;" for HE WHO GAVE THE THOUGHT IN OUR HEART HE LAID ALSO THE RESPONSIBILITY ON US THAT THIS THOUGHT SHOULD NOT REMAIN BARREN. He will raise, in due season, fellow-labourers who

      think
What others only dreamed about, and do
What others did but think, and glory in
What others dared but do.

Our work will begin small, and its progress will be, for a time, imperceptible ; but every inch of ground gained is lost to Rome and won to the Orthodox Reunion of Christendom.

OUTLINES OF THE CONSTITUTION OF THE ORTHODOX CATHOLIC CHURCH OF THE WEST.

I. THE Orthodox Catholic Church of the West being *essentially* the same as that of the East, both must profess *the same Faith*. Our Creed is therefore to be found in Peter Mogila's " Orthodox Confession of Faith of the Catholic and Apostolic Church," or in the Longer Catechism of the Russian Church (translated by Mr. Blackmore).

II. The East and the West must likewise have *the same fundamental Church-Constitution.* Therefore the Western Church accepts the Holy Canons of the seven œcumenical councils.

For further information see "*Die orthod. kath. Anschauung,*" p. 115 —126 ; and "*Po voprossu o soyedinenii tserkvey*" (On the question of the Reunion of Churches), St. Petersburg, 1866, p. 8 *seq.* The Russian author comprises my overtures in 16 items.

It would be a vain attempt to establish the Orthodox Church of the West, *Proprio Marte,* as an autokephalous Church. This would but be one more Schism. The first requisite of Western Orthodoxy is a *correct course in founding its Church.* Those who agree with the principles laid down in this book (the shortest expression of which is contained in the two points just exhibited) should commune with each other, and thus form a body of *petitioners* who would address themselves to "*the most Holy Governing Synod*" of the Russian Church in order to be, on the said basis, admitted into the Communion with that branch of the Orthodox Church, since that branch is nearer and more congenial to the West than any other branch of the Eastern Church (see above p. 54). Up to our formal reception into the Orthodox Church no administration of sacraments could take place, but we were only to join for private devotions, like catechumens, and in case of urgency, to apply to an Eastern Orthodox priest. As it will take a long time to settle all *minor details* of the question, our reception may not be deferred to such a moment, and it *cannot* be deferred by the Authorities of the Orthodox Church, if we pledge ourselves *not to retain or introduce anything Western which the Holy Governing Synod does not approve of.*

Thus the first thing of the Synod would be to license a Western priest validly ordained and conforming to Orthodoxy 1. to celebrate the Liturgy as found in the *Missale Romanum* (without the *Elevation* after the words of the Institution), of course the Masses of modern saints excluded ; 2. to confess the faithful; to administer the holy Communion *under both kinds;* to baptize *by trine immersion;* to solemnize the sacrament of matrimony ; and to dispense the sacrament of the Unction of the sick (not to be limited to the hopeless state of the dying). For the celebration of the Liturgy the Synod would supply an *Antiminsion.* The Liturgy and the other services would be held in the vernacular tongue, but the official language used in documents, Councils of the Western Church, &c., would remain the Latin. The sacerdotal garments (now partly curtailed and disfigured) to be restored to their primitive Western shape and simplicity. No opera-music, but the dignified Gregorian chant. Only *Icons* to be used in Church. The *Horæ canonicæ* to be purified from Romish stain ; and to be said in full length by the Regular Clergy (Monks), but "*ritu paschali*" by the Secular clergy.

The *indispensable* arrangements and regulations to be made by the Russian Church before founding the Orthodox Western Church, can therefore be greatly simplified by the clause " *salva Sanctæ Synodi approbatione,*" binding the Westerns in their proceedings. A long delay in founding the Western Church would be hurtful to the petitioners, as it precludes them from the sacramental grace and the other benefits of the Church, and it would endanger the great scheme of Church Union itself, since *procrastinated hopes grow dim.*

No Intercommunion but Reunion, Reunion with the Orthodox Catholic Church, a Reunion annihilating Schism and Heresy, Romanism and Protestantism, unbounded Tyranny and unbounded Liberty, a Reunion illustrating the great Gospel-principle : " *The Truth shall make you free !* "

Dear Anglo-Catholic Brethren, consider and reconsider your untenable position in the English Church, and look where God's finger points to.

> Uprouse ye now, brave brother band,
> With honest heart and working hand.
> We are but few, toil-tried, but true,
> And hearts beat high to dare and do ;
> Oh ! there be those that ache to see
> The day-dawn of our victory !

THE END.

JOHN CHILDS AND SON, PRINTERS.

www.ingramcontent.com/pod-product-compliance
Lightning Source LLC
Chambersburg PA
CBHW020902230426
43666CB00008B/1280